The History of the Netherlands

From Batavi to Golden Age

Introduction

Nestled in the northwestern corner of Europe lies a nation with a rich and diverse history, the Netherlands. Known for its picturesque landscapes, iconic windmills, and intricate canal systems, this small yet influential country has played a significant role in shaping the course of European history. As we embark on this journey to explore the history of the Netherlands, we will delve deep into its past, unraveling the intricate tapestry of events that have shaped its identity.

The story of the Netherlands is a story of resilience, innovation, and cultural exchange. From its earliest inhabitants, who settled along the fertile riverbanks and marshlands, to the flourishing trade routes of the medieval Hanseatic League and the maritime dominance of the Dutch Republic, this land has witnessed remarkable transformations.

Our exploration will take us through the ancient and medieval periods, where tribes such as the Batavi, Frisians, and Saxons left their mark on the Dutch landscape. We will uncover the impact of Roman rule and the enduring legacy of Charlemagne's Carolingian Empire. The Viking invasions and the rise of feudal lords will provide insights into the challenges and triumphs faced by the people of this region.

The emergence of Dutch cities, such as Amsterdam, Rotterdam, and Utrecht, as centers of commerce and culture during the Golden Age will be a focal point. We will also delve into the unique phenomenon of Tulip Mania and the Dutch East India Company (VOC), which transformed the Netherlands into a global trading power.

Throughout the chapters, we will explore the artistic brilliance of Rembrandt and the scientific achievements of Dutch scholars during the Golden Age. We will examine the impact of the Protestant Reformation and the Eighty Years' War, which led to the birth of Dutch independence.

The Dutch colonial legacy, including their presence in the Indonesian archipelago and involvement in the Atlantic Slave Trade, will be discussed in depth. We will also witness the turbulent times of the Napoleonic era and the subsequent restoration of independence.

Moving into the modern era, we will explore the post-World War II reconstruction and the development of the Dutch welfare state. We will learn about the enduring traditions, cuisine, and wildlife that make the Netherlands a unique and vibrant nation.

As we journey through the pages of this book, we will encounter the influential House of Orange-Nassau, the complexities of modern Dutch politics, and the enduring legacy of Dutch art, literature, and philosophy. Our exploration will encompass not only historical events but also the cultural, social, and economic forces that have shaped the Netherlands into the nation it is today.

The Netherlands is a land of contradictions and contrasts, where the struggle against water has led to remarkable engineering feats, and where a small nation has had a disproportionately significant impact on global affairs. Join us as we uncover the hidden gems and untold stories of this remarkable country, from its ancient beginnings to its modern-day prominence on the world stage.

The Geographical Tapestry: Land of the Low Countries

Nestled in the northwestern corner of Europe, the Netherlands, often referred to as the "Low Countries," is a country of unique geographical features and a landscape shaped by millennia of natural processes and human intervention.

The most distinctive characteristic of the Netherlands is its flatness. Approximately one-quarter of the country lies below sea level, making it one of the lowest-lying nations on Earth. This flat terrain is a result of its location in the vast North European Plain, a large expanse of relatively flat and fertile land that extends from France to Russia.

The country is often divided into three geographical regions. The first is the coastal region, known as the "Dutch Coast," which stretches along the North Sea. Here, you'll find a dynamic coastline with sandy beaches, dunes, and protective barriers such as dikes and dunes to combat the constant threat of sea-level rise and storms.

Moving inland, the second region is the "Polder Landscape." Polders are areas of land that have been drained and reclaimed from the sea, often characterized by a network of canals, dikes, and windmills. The Dutch have been reclaiming land from the sea for centuries, and these reclaimed polders are essential for agriculture and habitation.

The third region is the "Central Plateau," situated in the southern part of the country. This area is characterized by slightly higher elevations and rolling hills, offering a contrast to the flatness found in much of the Netherlands. The Limburg region, in the southeastern part of the country, is particularly known for its hilly terrain and is home to the highest point in the Netherlands, the Vaalserberg, which reaches a modest elevation of 322 meters (1,056 feet).

Water plays a central role in the Dutch landscape, with an intricate network of rivers, canals, and lakes crisscrossing the country. The major rivers that flow through the Netherlands include the Rhine, Meuse, and Scheldt. These waterways have historically been essential for transportation, trade, and agriculture.

Perhaps the most iconic feature of the Dutch landscape is its windmills. Windmills have been a part of Dutch culture for centuries and were historically used for various purposes, including grinding grain, draining polders, and sawing timber. While many traditional windmills are no longer in active use, they remain a symbol of Dutch heritage and can still be seen scattered across the countryside.

The Netherlands is also known for its extensive system of canals, which are used for transportation, irrigation, and flood control. Amsterdam, the capital city, is often referred to as the "Venice of the North" due to its intricate canal network.

To combat the ever-present threat of flooding, the Dutch have developed an intricate system of water management, including an extensive network of dikes, levees, and flood barriers. The Delta Works, a series of massive storm surge barriers and dams, is a testament to the Dutch commitment to keeping their low-lying lands safe from the encroaching sea.

In terms of size, the Netherlands is a relatively small country, covering an area of approximately 41,543 square kilometers (16,040 square miles). Despite its small size, it boasts a highly developed and densely populated landscape.

Cities and towns are closely packed together, and agriculture is highly efficient, making the most of the limited available land.

The Dutch relationship with water and their mastery over the landscape has not only shaped their geography but also their national identity. It is a land where water and land coexist in a delicate balance, where innovation and engineering have allowed a vibrant and thriving society to flourish amidst the challenges posed by its unique geographical tapestry.

Early Inhabitants: From Hunter-Gatherers to Settlers

The story of the early inhabitants of what is now the Netherlands dates back to the end of the last Ice Age, around 10,000 years ago. As the glaciers receded, a new landscape emerged in the region that would become the Low Countries. These early inhabitants were hunter-gatherers, relying on the abundant natural resources of the fertile land.

Evidence of their presence can be found in archaeological sites scattered throughout the Netherlands. These sites reveal a rich tapestry of life during the Mesolithic and Neolithic periods. The people of this era lived in small, nomadic groups, moving in search of food and resources. They were skilled hunters and gatherers, relying on a diet that included game such as wild boar, deer, and a variety of fish from the rivers and lakes.

The archaeological record also shows evidence of the tools and implements these early inhabitants used in their daily lives. Stone tools, such as flint blades and arrowheads, were crafted with precision and skill, a testament to the resourcefulness of these ancient people.

As time passed and the climate continued to warm, the landscape of the Netherlands underwent significant changes. Dense forests covered much of the land, and the people of the Neolithic period began to engage in agriculture. They cleared the forests to make way for fields and domesticated animals, marking the transition from hunter-gatherer societies to settled farming communities.

One of the most significant archaeological discoveries from this era is the Funnelbeaker Culture, named after the distinctive funnel-shaped pottery vessels found at their sites. These early farmers practiced a mix of agriculture and animal husbandry, relying on crops like wheat, barley, and flax, as well as herding cattle, sheep, and pigs.

The transition to settled farming communities brought about profound changes in the social structure of these early societies. Villages emerged, with houses built from timber and thatch. These communities likely had a degree of specialization, with some individuals specializing in agriculture, others in animal husbandry, and still others in crafts such as pottery and weaving.

The people of the Funnelbeaker Culture were not isolated; they engaged in trade and cultural exchange with neighboring regions. This contact led to the exchange of goods, ideas, and technologies, enriching the cultural fabric of the early Dutch inhabitants.

The megalithic monuments known as dolmens and hunebedden also mark this period in the Netherlands' history. These massive stone structures were built as tombs and have captivated the imagination of modern-day observers, offering a glimpse into the beliefs and practices of the people who constructed them.

It is important to note that the early history of the Netherlands is intertwined with the broader European context. The movement of peoples, the spread of agricultural practices, and the development of early civilizations all played a role in shaping the landscape and culture of the Low Countries.

The Rise of the Batavi: Ancient Dutch Tribes

In the early centuries of the Common Era, the Low Countries, now known as the Netherlands, were inhabited by various tribal groups. Among these, the Batavi stand out as a notable and enigmatic people whose presence and actions in the region left a lasting impact on the history of the Dutch tribes.

The Batavi were a Germanic tribe that settled in the area that is now the Netherlands, particularly in the regions of Gelderland and South Holland. Their exact origins are a subject of scholarly debate, but it is generally believed that they were of Germanic stock, possibly originating from the area around the Rhine River. The Batavi's name itself suggests a connection to water, as "Batavi" is thought to be related to the Old Germanic word for "boat."

One of the earliest mentions of the Batavi comes from the Roman historian Tacitus, who documented their presence in his work "Germania" around 98 CE. Tacitus described the Batavi as a proud and formidable tribe, known for their warrior culture and skill in battle. They were considered exceptional horsemen and often served as elite cavalry units in the Roman army.

The Batavi's relationship with the Roman Empire is a key aspect of their history. During the late 1st century CE, they formed an alliance with the Romans and played a significant role in the Roman conquest of Britain. The Batavian revolt of 69-70 CE, led by Julius Civilis, marked a brief period of rebellion against Roman rule but ultimately ended in Roman victory.

Throughout their history, the Batavi maintained a semi-autonomous status within the Roman Empire. They were granted certain privileges and allowed to govern themselves to a degree. This autonomy was in part due to their military prowess and the strategic importance of their territory along the Rhine River, which served as a vital frontier for the Roman Empire.

The Batavi's military contributions extended beyond their alliance with Rome. Their skilled warriors were sought after as mercenaries by various Roman emperors. The Batavi played a crucial role in the defense of the Roman Empire's borders against external threats, including the Germanic tribes to the east.

While their military achievements are well-documented, less is known about the Batavi's daily life and culture. They likely practiced agriculture and animal husbandry, like many other Germanic tribes of the time. Their settlements were likely centered around fortified villages, and they had a tribal leadership structure.

Over time, as the Roman Empire faced internal and external pressures, the Batavi's autonomy waned, and their identity became increasingly Romanized. The collapse of the Western Roman Empire in the 5th century CE marked a turning point in the history of the Batavi and the entire region. As Roman authority diminished, various Germanic tribes, including the Franks, invaded and settled in the Low Countries.

The Batavi, like many other ancient tribes, gradually faded from historical records, leaving behind a legacy of warrior prowess and contributions to the Roman Empire's military might. While their precise fate remains a subject of historical speculation, their existence and impact on the ancient Dutch tribes are undeniable.

Roman Rule and Influence in the Netherlands

The influence of the Roman Empire in what is now the Netherlands left an indelible mark on the region's history and culture. The period of Roman rule in the Low Countries, which roughly corresponds to the 1st through the 4th centuries CE, was a time of transformation and integration.

The Romans first established a presence in the Netherlands as part of their broader efforts to expand their empire into northern Europe. The conquest of Gaul, led by Julius Caesar in the 1st century BCE, paved the way for Roman influence in the region. The lands of the Batavi, Frisii, and other indigenous tribes became part of the Roman province of Germania Inferior, with modern-day Nijmegen serving as the capital.

One of the key features of Roman rule was the construction of an extensive network of roads and fortifications. The Roman road known as the "Via Belgica" connected the Low Countries with the rest of the Roman Empire, facilitating trade, communication, and the movement of troops. Forts and watchtowers were established along the borders, including the Limes, a line of defenses along the Rhine River, which marked the northernmost extent of the Roman Empire.

Urbanization was another hallmark of Roman influence. Cities such as Utrecht, Maastricht, and Nijmegen began to develop as administrative and economic centers. These cities featured Roman-style architecture, including bathhouses, temples, and forums, showcasing the Romans' architectural prowess.

The Romanization of the local population had a profound impact on the Dutch tribes. Roman law and governance systems were introduced, and Latin became the language of administration. The indigenous peoples adopted Roman customs and lifestyles, and trade with the wider Roman Empire enriched the region's material culture.

Roman religion also left its mark, with the worship of Roman gods and goddesses becoming prevalent. Temples and altars dedicated to deities like Mercury, Mars, and Jupiter were erected in the cities, reflecting the syncretism between Roman and indigenous beliefs.

One of the most iconic aspects of Roman culture introduced to the Netherlands was the Roman bathhouse. The ancient city of Heerlen boasts one of the best-preserved Roman bathhouses in the region, providing a glimpse into the daily life and hygiene practices of the time.

The Roman period in the Low Countries was not without its challenges. The Batavian Revolt, led by Julius Civilis in 69-70 CE, marked a brief period of rebellion against Roman rule. Although the revolt was ultimately suppressed, it revealed the tensions that existed between the indigenous peoples and their Roman overlords.

As the Roman Empire faced internal and external pressures, including invasions by Germanic tribes, the Roman presence in the Netherlands began to wane. The decline of the Western Roman Empire in the 4th and 5th centuries CE signaled the end of Roman rule in the region. The Roman forts along the Limes were abandoned, and the Roman way of life gradually gave way to the influence of incoming Germanic tribes.

While the Roman period in the Netherlands may have been relatively brief in terms of centuries, its impact was lasting. The legacy of Roman roads, architecture, governance, and culture can still be seen and felt in the Netherlands today, serving as a testament to the enduring influence of one of history's greatest empires on the ancient Dutch landscape.

Frisians and Saxons: Germanic Roots

The history of the Netherlands is deeply intertwined with the Germanic tribes that inhabited the region during ancient and medieval times. Among these tribes, the Frisians and Saxons played pivotal roles in shaping the cultural and social fabric of what would become the Low Countries.

The Frisians, a Germanic people with a long and storied history, inhabited the coastal regions of what is now the northern Netherlands, parts of Germany, and Denmark. The origins of the Frisians are somewhat obscure, but they are believed to have migrated to the coastal areas around the 1st century BCE. They were seafaring people, known for their maritime skills and the construction of terpen, or artificial mounds, as protection against rising sea levels and flooding.

The Frisians had a strong sense of regional identity and were organized into loosely connected tribes, each with its own leadership and customs. They were not unified under a single ruler but rather maintained a degree of autonomy. Their language, Old Frisian, is considered one of the earliest forms of the Germanic languages.

Trade and commerce were integral to the Frisian way of life. They engaged in long-distance trade, connecting the North Sea region with the wider European world. Their trading ventures extended as far as Britain and the Baltic Sea, and their seafaring prowess allowed them to establish a significant presence in trade networks.

The Frisians' interactions with the Roman Empire were complex. While they were not directly under Roman rule, they engaged in trade and cultural exchange with the Romans. Roman coins and artifacts have been found in

Frisian archaeological sites, attesting to their connections with the Roman world.

The Saxons, another prominent Germanic tribe, inhabited the eastern and central parts of what is now the Netherlands, as well as parts of Germany. Like the Frisians, the origins of the Saxons are somewhat shrouded in the mists of time. They were known for their farming and cattle-raising activities, living in small agricultural communities.

The Saxons had a decentralized social and political structure, with tribes ruled by chieftains. They, too, were seafarers, with access to the North Sea and the rivers that crisscrossed the region. Their interactions with neighboring tribes, including the Franks and the Frisians, were marked by both cooperation and conflict.

The spread of Christianity into the lands inhabited by the Frisians and Saxons marked a significant turning point in their history. Missionaries from the Christianized Franks, such as Saint Boniface, played key roles in converting these Germanic tribes to Christianity during the early medieval period. This religious transformation had profound cultural and social implications, shaping the religious landscape of the Low Countries.

The Frisians and Saxons left behind a legacy of cultural and linguistic influences that can still be seen today. Elements of their languages and customs are preserved in the modern Dutch language and culture. Their historical presence and contributions serve as a testament to the rich tapestry of the Netherlands' Germanic roots, providing a deeper understanding of the nation's heritage and identity.

Viking Invasions: Raiders of the Northern Seas

The Viking invasions that swept across northern Europe during the late 8th to the early 11th centuries were a defining period in the history of the Netherlands. These seafaring Scandinavian warriors, known as Vikings, embarked on daring raids, explorations, and conquests that left a significant mark on the regions they encountered, including the Low Countries.

The Vikings, originating from the lands of modern-day Norway, Sweden, and Denmark, were skilled sailors and navigators. Their longships, characterized by their shallow draft and flexible design, enabled them to traverse both open seas and shallow rivers with ease. These vessels were the key to their rapid mobility and the success of their incursions.

The first recorded Viking raids on the Netherlands occurred in the late 8th century, with coastal towns and monasteries along the North Sea bearing the brunt of their attacks. The Vikings targeted these settlements for their wealth, valuables, and livestock. They struck swiftly and ferociously, often catching the local populations off guard.

One of the most significant Viking invasions in the Netherlands occurred in 834 when a Viking fleet, led by the chieftain Rorik, ravaged the Frisian coast. This incursion marked the beginning of a period of intermittent Viking presence in the region. Over the subsequent decades, the Vikings established temporary bases along the Dutch coast, using them as launch points for further raids. The Vikings were not merely raiders; they were also traders and explorers. Their voyages took them along the rivers and waterways of the Netherlands, enabling them to trade with local populations and penetrate deeper into the continent. This interaction had a lasting impact on the exchange of goods, culture, and ideas in the region.

In the 9th century, the Vikings' presence intensified, with the establishment of more permanent settlements, or "wics," in areas like Dorestad (modern-day Wijk bij Duurstede) and Tiel. These wics served as centers of trade and economic activity, connecting the Vikings with the local Frisian and Frankish populations.

As the Viking Age progressed, the Netherlands saw a shift from raiding to conquest. The Vikings began to seek territorial control and engaged in conflicts with local rulers and neighboring powers. One of the most famous Viking leaders of this era was Rollo, who would later become the first Duke of Normandy in France. Rollo's Viking forces settled in the northern part of the region now known as Normandy, which takes its name from the Norsemen.

By the early 10th century, the Vikings' presence in the Netherlands began to wane as their focus shifted to other regions of Europe. The influence of Frankish rulers and the spread of Christianity played a role in reducing Viking activity in the Low Countries. The consolidation of regional power also made it more challenging for Viking incursions to continue.

Despite their reputation as raiders and invaders, the Vikings left a lasting legacy in the Netherlands. Their presence contributed to the development of trade networks, the exchange of cultural influences, and the evolution of the Dutch language. The memory of their exploits and the impact of their era are still evident in the historical and archaeological records of the region, serving as a reminder of the Vikings' role as formidable and influential figures in Dutch history.

Charlemagne's Carolingian Empire and the Dutch Connection

The era of Charlemagne, also known as Charles the Great or Carolus Magnus, represents a pivotal chapter in the history of the Netherlands and its connection to the broader European landscape. Charlemagne, who ruled as the King of the Franks and later became the Emperor of the Carolingian Empire from 768 to 814 CE, left an indelible mark on the Low Countries.

Charlemagne's reign marked a period of expansion and consolidation of power in Western Europe. He aimed to revive the idea of the Roman Empire and establish a centralized and Christianized European realm. This ambitious vision had far-reaching consequences for the Low Countries.

The region now known as the Netherlands was part of the Carolingian Empire, encompassing present-day Belgium, parts of northern France, and parts of Germany. During Charlemagne's reign, this territory was under the administration of a series of Carolingian officials known as "missi dominici," who were responsible for ensuring the king's authority and overseeing local governance.

Charlemagne recognized the strategic importance of the Low Countries, given their proximity to the North Sea, which facilitated trade and communication with Scandinavia, England, and other parts of Northern Europe. The network of rivers and waterways in the region also played a vital role in transportation and commerce.

One of Charlemagne's notable achievements was his efforts to Christianize the Low Countries. He encouraged the establishment of monasteries and churches, promoting the spread of Christianity among the indigenous population. The monastic center of Utrecht, for example, became an important religious and educational hub during this period.

The Carolingian Renaissance, a revival of learning and culture inspired by Charlemagne, also reached the Low Countries. Monasteries in the region became centers of scriptoria, where monks copied and preserved classical and Christian texts. This intellectual revival contributed to the preservation of knowledge and culture during a tumultuous era.

The Carolingian Empire's administrative and legal systems influenced the development of governance in the Low Countries. The division of the empire into counties, each ruled by a count, established a system of local administration that endured for centuries. The Counts of Holland and other regional rulers were descendants of the Carolingian system.

Charlemagne's legacy extended to the establishment of a standardized currency, the Carolingian denarius, which facilitated trade and economic development in the region. The expansion of agriculture and the development of trade routes contributed to the prosperity of the Low Countries during this period.

However, Charlemagne's death in 814 marked the beginning of a period of fragmentation in the Carolingian Empire. His grandsons divided the empire into separate realms, including the eastern and western portions of the Low Countries. This fragmentation led to the emergence of regional powers and the eventual formation of distinct entities such as the County of Flanders and the Duchy of Brabant.

Despite the dissolution of the Carolingian Empire, Charlemagne's legacy endured in the collective memory of the Low Countries. His efforts to promote Christianity, education, and governance left an indelible mark on the region, shaping its cultural, religious, and political landscape for centuries to come. The Dutch connection to Charlemagne's empire serves as a testament to the enduring influence of this remarkable ruler on the history of the Netherlands.

Feudal Lords and Medieval Estates: Dutch Society

The medieval period brought significant changes to Dutch society, marked by the rise of feudalism and the emergence of a complex social structure. During this era, which spanned roughly from the 9th to the 15th century, the Low Countries underwent transformations that shaped the socioeconomic landscape and set the stage for the nation's future development.

At the heart of medieval Dutch society was the feudal system, a hierarchical arrangement that defined the relationships between landowners, lords, and serfs. Land was the primary source of wealth and power, and it was often granted by the monarch or a higher-ranking noble to vassals in exchange for military service and loyalty.

The feudal lords, or nobility, played a central role in Dutch society. They held vast estates and exercised authority over the lands and the people who lived on them. The most prominent among these nobles were the dukes, counts, and barons, who governed the various regions of the Low Countries. Notable examples include the Counts of Holland and the Dukes of Burgundy, who exerted significant influence over the territory.

Beneath the nobility, the hierarchy extended to lesser lords, knights, and local officials who administered justice and collected taxes on behalf of their feudal superiors. Knights, in particular, were the warrior class of the medieval Dutch society, often owing military service and allegiance to higher-ranking lords.

Peasants formed the largest segment of the population during the medieval period. They were the backbone of the agrarian economy, working the land and producing food and resources essential for survival. Peasants were typically bound to the land they worked and were subject to the authority of the local lord. Their lives were marked by hard labor and a commitment to their feudal obligations.

The medieval Dutch urban centers began to flourish during this period. Towns and cities emerged as hubs of trade, commerce, and culture. Craftsmen, merchants, and artisans formed guilds to protect their interests and maintain standards of quality. These guilds played a crucial role in shaping the economies of the urban centers.

Medieval Dutch society was also influenced by the Catholic Church, which held considerable power and influence. Monasteries and religious institutions played a central role in providing education, preserving knowledge, and offering spiritual guidance. The clergy, including bishops and abbots, wielded significant authority in both religious and secular matters.

The rise of medieval estates, or representative bodies, was another notable development during this period. These estates consisted of three classes: the clergy, the nobility, and the commons. They convened to advise and consent on matters of governance, taxation, and legislation, providing a rudimentary form of representative government.

The medieval Dutch legal system was based on customary law and feudal obligations. Local courts administered justice, with feudal lords and their representatives presiding over cases. The legal codes and traditions varied from region to region, reflecting the decentralized nature of medieval Dutch society.

As the medieval period progressed, the Low Countries became increasingly entwined with wider European events.

The Hundred Years' War, the Crusades, and the conflicts between the Dukes of Burgundy and other European powers all had repercussions in the Dutch lands. These events influenced the political dynamics and cultural exchanges that shaped the evolving Dutch identity.

In summary, the medieval period in the Low Countries was characterized by a hierarchical social structure, with feudal lords, knights, and peasants forming the core of society. The emergence of urban centers, the influence of the Catholic Church, and the development of representative estates were significant aspects of medieval Dutch society. These developments laid the foundation for the nation's future political, economic, and cultural evolution.

Medieval Trade Routes: Hanseatic League and Beyond

The medieval period witnessed a flourishing of trade and commerce in Europe, and the Low Countries, with their strategic location at the crossroads of northern and western Europe, played a pivotal role in this dynamic economic landscape. This chapter explores the intricate network of medieval trade routes that crisscrossed the region, with a focus on the Hanseatic League and the broader context of medieval commerce.

The Hanseatic League, often referred to simply as the Hansa, was a powerful and influential trading alliance of cities and merchant guilds that emerged during the late medieval period. The league's origins can be traced back to the 12th century, with the first formal Hanseatic Diet held in 1356. It initially comprised cities in the Baltic and North Sea regions, but it later expanded to include numerous cities across northern Europe, including several in the Low Countries.

The Hanseatic League had its headquarters in the German city of Lübeck, but it included several prominent Dutch members, such as Bruges, Ghent, and Amsterdam. These cities formed part of the Hanseatic trading network that extended from the Baltic Sea to the North Sea and beyond. The league's primary objectives were to promote and protect its members' trade interests, and it achieved this through a combination of economic cooperation and military power.

The Hansa was instrumental in facilitating the trade of goods such as grain, timber, fish, and salt, which were vital commodities in medieval Europe. Its ships, known as cog ships, plied the waters of the North and Baltic Seas, connecting the Hanseatic cities and fostering a thriving exchange of goods and ideas.

One of the most notable features of the Hanseatic League was its ability to establish trading posts and kontors in foreign cities, including those in the Low Countries. The kontors served as hubs for Hanseatic merchants, where they could conduct business, store goods, and negotiate trade agreements. The kontor in Bruges, for example, was a vital center of Hanseatic trade in the Low Countries.

The Hanseatic League's influence extended well beyond economic matters. It played a significant role in shaping the legal and political landscape of the regions where it operated. The league's merchants had their own legal code, known as the Law of the Hansa, which governed trade disputes and contractual agreements. Additionally, the league often negotiated directly with monarchs and rulers, asserting its considerable political clout.

While the Hanseatic League was a dominant force in medieval trade, it was by no means the only one. The Low Countries were also home to a multitude of other trade routes and associations. The Rhine River, which flowed through the region, served as a vital trade artery, connecting inland cities with coastal ports and facilitating the movement of goods.

The Low Countries were known for their bustling markets and fairs, where merchants from all corners of Europe converged to exchange goods. The Champagne fairs in northern France, for instance, drew traders from the Low Countries and beyond, creating a vibrant nexus of commerce.

Additionally, the rise of medieval towns and cities in the Low Countries spurred economic growth. Urbanization brought about the development of craft guilds, which organized and regulated the production of goods. Flemish and Dutch cities became renowned for their skilled craftsmen and artisans, producing high-quality textiles, ceramics, and other luxury items.

The medieval trade routes and networks that intersected in the Low Countries played a pivotal role in the economic, political, and cultural development of the region. The Hanseatic League, with its far-reaching influence, was a central player in this intricate web of commerce, leaving a lasting legacy in the annals of Dutch history. The medieval trade routes laid the foundation for the economic prosperity and global trade relationships that would continue to evolve in the centuries to come.

The Golden Age of Dutch Cities

The 17th century, often referred to as the Golden Age of the Dutch Republic, was a remarkable period in the history of the Netherlands. During this era, the Dutch cities experienced unprecedented economic prosperity, cultural flourishing, and global influence. The Golden Age was characterized by a unique combination of factors that propelled the Dutch Republic to the forefront of European politics, trade, and culture.

At the heart of the Dutch Golden Age were the cities, which served as the epicenters of economic and cultural activity. Amsterdam, in particular, emerged as a global economic powerhouse. The city's strategic location along the North Sea and its well-developed harbor made it a hub for international trade.

The Dutch East India Company (VOC) and the Dutch West India Company (WIC) played pivotal roles in the economic success of Dutch cities during this period. The VOC, established in 1602, was instrumental in establishing Dutch dominance in the lucrative spice trade in the East Indies. Amsterdam served as the headquarters of the VOC, and the company's operations extended to Asia, Africa, and the Americas.

The WIC, founded in 1621, focused on trade and colonization in the Americas, particularly in areas like New Netherland (present-day New York) and the Caribbean. Dutch cities like Amsterdam and New Amsterdam (now New York City) became centers for trade, commerce, and settlement in the New World.

The Dutch mastery of maritime trade routes allowed them to amass significant wealth. Dutch cities teemed with merchants, traders, and entrepreneurs who engaged in a wide range of economic activities, from shipbuilding and ship repair to textile production and banking. The city of Amsterdam, in particular, became a financial powerhouse, with the establishment of the Amsterdam Stock Exchange in 1602, one of the earliest stock exchanges in the world.

The economic prosperity of Dutch cities had a profound impact on their urban development. The cities underwent ambitious expansion projects, with canals being dug and urban planning prioritizing both functionality and aesthetics. Amsterdam's concentric canal ring, built during this period, is a UNESCO World Heritage site and a testament to the city's commitment to urban planning and beauty.

Art and culture flourished during the Dutch Golden Age, with cities like Amsterdam, Haarlem, and Delft becoming centers of artistic innovation. Renowned painters such as Rembrandt van Rijn, Johannes Vermeer, and Frans Hals produced masterpieces that continue to be celebrated today. Dutch literature, theater, and philosophy also experienced significant growth.

Dutch cities were known for their tolerance and openness, attracting individuals from various backgrounds and beliefs. This diversity contributed to a rich cultural tapestry that promoted intellectual exchange and innovation. The city of Leiden, for example, was home to the University of Leiden, a leading center for learning and scholarship.

The Dutch Golden Age also witnessed the rise of a vibrant middle class, which played a vital role in the country's prosperity. This middle class, consisting of merchants, artisans, and professionals, had a strong influence on the political landscape. The Dutch Republic's political system was characterized by a unique form of government known as the "Dutch Republic's executive-oligarchic system." It combined elements of oligarchy, republicanism, and federalism, with significant power vested in city governments and merchant regents.

The Golden Age's cultural and intellectual achievements extended to the realm of science and exploration. Dutch scholars like Christiaan Huygens and Antonie van Leeuwenhoek made groundbreaking contributions to fields such as astronomy and microbiology. Dutch explorers and navigators charted new territories and played a crucial role in the development of global maritime exploration.

The Dutch cities' prosperity and global influence, however, were not without challenges and conflicts. The Eighty Years' War with Spain, which led to the recognition of Dutch independence in 1648, was a pivotal event in the Dutch Republic's history. The war was marked by significant military campaigns and diplomatic negotiations, ultimately resulting in the Treaty of Westphalia and the formal recognition of the Dutch Republic's sovereignty.

The Dutch Golden Age began to wane in the latter half of the 17th century, as internal and external factors began to erode the republic's dominant position. Economic competition from other European nations, conflicts like the Anglo-Dutch Wars, and the decline of the VOC and WIC all contributed to the Netherlands' changing fortunes.

Nonetheless, the legacy of the Dutch Golden Age endures. Dutch cities like Amsterdam, Haarlem, and Utrecht continue to be celebrated for their cultural heritage and historical significance. The artistic, scientific, and economic achievements of this era continue to shape the identity of the Netherlands and serve as a testament to the resilience, innovation, and creativity of Dutch society during its Golden Age.

The Dike Builders: Managing Water and Land

The Netherlands, a nation known for its intricate network of waterways, canals, and low-lying landscapes, owes much of its existence to the relentless efforts of its people in managing water and land. The history of the Dutch and their relationship with water is a testament to their ingenuity, resilience, and determination.

For centuries, the Dutch have faced the constant threat of flooding from the North Sea and the numerous rivers that crisscross their territory. These natural waterways, while offering opportunities for trade and transportation, also brought the risk of inundation. The need to protect their homes and fertile farmlands from the encroaching waters led to the development of one of the most iconic features of the Dutch landscape: the dike.

Dike building in the Netherlands dates back to Roman times, but it was during the Middle Ages that the construction of dikes became a coordinated effort. The medieval period saw the emergence of local water boards or "waterschappen," which were responsible for the maintenance and construction of dikes. These early dike builders utilized basic tools and the collective labor of communities to erect protective embankments.

The construction of dikes required meticulous planning and engineering. Dikes needed to be tall and sturdy enough to withstand the force of the sea and river waters. Ingenious systems of sluices, locks, and windmills were employed to manage water levels and drainage, helping to reclaim land and protect against floods. Windmills, in particular, became a symbol of Dutch engineering prowess and played a crucial role in pumping water from low-lying polders.

One of the most famous examples of Dutch dike building is the Zuiderzee Works, a monumental project undertaken in the early 20th century. This ambitious endeavor aimed to transform the Zuiderzee, a large, shallow inlet of the North Sea, into a freshwater lake and fertile farmland. The construction of the Afsluitdijk (Enclosure Dam) in 1932 effectively closed off the Zuiderzee from the sea, creating the Ijsselmeer and marking a significant achievement in Dutch water management.

The Dutch have also harnessed the power of water to create new land through a process known as land reclamation. Polders, or areas of land reclaimed from bodies of water, have been a hallmark of Dutch landscape engineering. The famous Beemster Polder, established in 1612, is recognized as the first large-scale land reclamation project in the world. It exemplifies the Dutch ability to turn water into arable land, contributing to the nation's agricultural productivity.

The maintenance of dikes and the battle against water remain ongoing efforts in the Netherlands. The Delta Works, a series of dams, sluices, locks, dikes, and storm surge barriers, were constructed after the devastating North Sea Flood of 1953, which claimed over 1,800 lives. These massive engineering feats were designed to protect the vulnerable southwestern provinces from future inundations.

In addition to their practical function, dikes have also become integral to Dutch culture and identity. The famous Dutch saying, "God created the world, but the Dutch created the Netherlands," underscores the nation's enduring commitment to land reclamation and water management.

Water management in the Netherlands extends beyond dikes and polders. The country's system of canals and waterways, dating back to the Dutch Golden Age, has facilitated trade, transportation, and drainage. Cities like

Amsterdam are renowned for their picturesque canals, which are not only scenic but also serve as part of an intricate flood control system.

In recent years, the Dutch have continued to innovate in water management. The concept of "room for the river" involves creating more space for rivers to flood safely during periods of high water, reducing the risk of catastrophic inundations. Sustainable approaches to water management, such as green roofs and urban planning that integrates water storage, are gaining traction in Dutch cities.

The Dutch have indeed mastered the art of balancing their relationship with water. Their expertise in dike building, land reclamation, and water management has not only protected their homeland but has also positioned them as global leaders in water engineering and resilience.

Flanders and the Dutch Renaissance

The Dutch Renaissance, a cultural and artistic movement that swept through the Low Countries during the 16th and 17th centuries, left an indelible mark on the region's history. At the heart of this Renaissance was Flanders, a historic region that played a central role in the blossoming of Dutch art, culture, and intellectual pursuits.

The Dutch Renaissance was characterized by a revival of interest in the classical arts and a departure from the medieval traditions that had dominated the preceding centuries. Flanders, with its thriving urban centers and affluent merchant class, provided fertile ground for the Renaissance to take root and flourish.

Flanders, encompassing modern-day Belgium and parts of northern France and the Netherlands, was a vibrant hub of trade and commerce during this period. Cities like Bruges, Ghent, and Antwerp were among the wealthiest and most cosmopolitan in Europe, attracting not only merchants but also scholars, artists, and craftsmen from across the continent.

One of the defining features of the Dutch Renaissance was the emphasis on humanism, a scholarly movement that celebrated the study of classical texts and the development of human potential. Humanist thinkers like Erasmus of Rotterdam, who was born in what is now the Netherlands, played a crucial role in promoting the ideals of humanism. Their writings and ideas encouraged a shift toward critical thinking, education, and the pursuit of knowledge.

Art and architecture thrived in Flanders during the Renaissance. The Flemish Primitives, a group of painters active in the 15th and early 16th centuries, made significant contributions to the development of realistic and finely detailed oil painting techniques. Artists like Jan van Eyck, Rogier van der Weyden, and Hans Memling created exquisite works of art that captured the world with meticulous precision.

Flemish painting during the Renaissance was characterized by its attention to detail, use of vibrant colors, and the mastery of light and shadow. The development of oil painting techniques allowed for greater depth and realism in art, enabling artists to create lifelike portraits, landscapes, and religious scenes.

The Ghent Altarpiece, created by the van Eyck brothers, is considered one of the masterpieces of Flemish Renaissance art. This complex and intricate polyptych is renowned for its detailed representation of religious subjects and its use of vibrant pigments.

In addition to painting, Flemish architecture experienced a Renaissance revival, with a focus on classical elements such as columns, pilasters, and arches. The Stadhuis (City Hall) in Antwerp, designed by Cornelis Floris de Vriendt, is a notable example of Flemish Renaissance architecture, characterized by its ornate façade and richly decorated interiors.

The Dutch Renaissance was not confined to the arts; it extended to literature, science, and philosophy. Humanist scholars like Desiderius Erasmus produced influential writings that promoted humanist ideals and intellectual inquiry. Erasmus's "In Praise of Folly" critiqued societal and religious norms with wit and satire, challenging established authorities.

Scientific progress also marked the Dutch Renaissance. The era saw advancements in navigation, cartography, and astronomy, contributing to the Dutch Republic's status as a maritime and trading powerhouse. Gerardus Mercator, a Flemish cartographer, developed the Mercator projection, a groundbreaking map projection that revolutionized navigation.

The Dutch Renaissance era also witnessed significant developments in printing and publishing. The invention of the printing press by Johannes Gutenberg in the 15th century had a profound impact on the dissemination of knowledge. Dutch cities like Antwerp became major centers for the production and distribution of books, fostering the spread of ideas throughout Europe.

Religious and political developments during the Dutch Renaissance era were marked by the Protestant Reformation and the Eighty Years' War for Dutch independence from Spanish rule. The Reformation led to religious divisions in the Low Countries, with Calvinism gaining a foothold in some regions, while Catholicism remained dominant in others.

The Dutch Revolt, which began in the late 16th century, was a struggle for independence from Spanish Habsburg rule. It culminated in the Treaty of Westphalia in 1648, which recognized the Dutch Republic as an independent nation. This period of political upheaval had profound cultural and artistic implications, as it fostered a sense of national identity and pride.

The Dutch Golden Age, which followed the Dutch Renaissance, built upon the cultural and economic foundations established during this earlier period. The Dutch Republic became a dominant European power, and its cities, including Amsterdam, thrived as centers of trade, art, and culture.

The Protestant Reformation in the Netherlands

The Protestant Reformation, a profound religious and cultural movement that swept across Europe in the 16th century, had a significant impact on the Netherlands. This chapter explores the complex and transformative history of the Protestant Reformation in the Low Countries, which ultimately led to religious divisions, political upheaval, and the emergence of the Dutch Republic.

The roots of the Reformation in the Netherlands can be traced back to the late 15th century when the humanist ideas of scholars like Desiderius Erasmus began to gain prominence. Erasmus, a Dutchman himself, was a critical thinker who questioned the practices and corruption within the Catholic Church. His writings, including "In Praise of Folly," challenged established religious norms and contributed to a climate of intellectual inquiry.

However, it was the arrival of Martin Luther's ideas from Germany that ignited the flames of the Reformation in the Netherlands. Luther's 95 Theses, published in 1517, criticized the sale of indulgences and questioned the authority of the Catholic Church. Luther's writings were quickly disseminated throughout Europe, including the Low Countries, thanks to the recent invention of the printing press.

The spread of Lutheran ideas found fertile ground in the Netherlands, where dissatisfaction with the Catholic Church's practices and the desire for religious reform had been brewing for some time. The 16th century witnessed the rise of Protestant movements, with Lutheranism and Anabaptism gaining followers in various regions.

The most significant and enduring branch of the Reformation in the Netherlands, however, was Calvinism. John Calvin's teachings, which emphasized predestination, the authority of Scripture, and the importance of a personal relationship with God, resonated deeply with many Dutch believers. Calvinist ideas were disseminated through printed materials, sermons, and discussions, contributing to the rapid spread of Reformed Protestantism.

The early 16th century also saw the emergence of Protestant martyrs in the Netherlands. Men like Jan de Bakker and Hendrik Vos were among the first to be executed for their adherence to Lutheran beliefs. These martyrdoms, rather than suppressing the Protestant movement, galvanized its followers and strengthened their resolve.

In 1566, a pivotal event known as the Iconoclastic Fury, or the Beeldenstorm, occurred. Calvinist mobs and iconoclasts targeted Catholic churches and monasteries, vandalizing and destroying religious images and artifacts. The Beeldenstorm was a manifestation of the growing tensions between Catholics and Protestants and marked a turning point in the Reformation's impact on Dutch society.

The political situation in the Netherlands added further complexity to the Reformation. The region was under the control of the Habsburg monarchy, led by King Philip II of Spain. Philip's unwavering commitment to Catholicism and his attempts to suppress Protestantism led to growing discontent among the Dutch population.

The Dutch Revolt, which began in the late 16th century, was a direct result of the religious and political tensions in the Netherlands. The conflict, known as the Eighty Years' War, saw Dutch rebels fighting for independence from Spanish Habsburg rule. The Reformation and the desire for religious freedom became intertwined with the struggle for national sovereignty.

The Dutch Revolt led to a significant political development: the establishment of the Union of Utrecht in 1579. This union brought together several northern provinces of the Netherlands and formalized their commitment to resist Spanish rule and uphold the principles of religious tolerance. The Union of Utrecht marked a critical step toward the formation of the Dutch Republic.

In 1581, the Act of Abjuration, also known as the Plakkaat van Verlatinghe, declared the independence of the northern provinces from Philip II's rule. The act stated that a ruler who failed to protect the rights and liberties of the people could be deposed. This declaration of independence was a precursor to the formal recognition of the Dutch Republic in the Treaty of Westphalia in 1648.

Throughout the turbulent period of the Dutch Revolt, Calvinism became the dominant religious tradition in the newly emerging Dutch Republic. The Reformed Church, shaped by Calvinist theology, played a central role in the religious and cultural life of the nation.

The Protestant Reformation had a profound and lasting impact on the Netherlands. It not only led to religious divisions but also contributed to the emergence of the Dutch Republic as a bastion of religious tolerance and political independence in Europe.

Eighty Years' War: Birth of Dutch Independence

The Eighty Years' War, also known as the Dutch War of Independence, was a protracted and tumultuous conflict that spanned from 1568 to 1648. It marked a defining moment in Dutch history, as it culminated in the recognition of the Dutch Republic as an independent nation and laid the foundation for modern-day Netherlands. This chapter explores the multifaceted and complex series of events that led to the birth of Dutch independence.

The roots of the Eighty Years' War can be traced back to several interconnected factors. One of the primary catalysts was the religious turmoil of the 16th century. The spread of Protestantism, fueled by the ideas of reformers like Martin Luther and John Calvin, had gained a significant following in the Low Countries. However, the region was under the rule of the Habsburg monarchy, led by King Philip II of Spain, who was staunchly Catholic and sought to suppress Protestantism.

Religious tensions ran high, as the Catholic authorities initiated measures to enforce religious conformity and root out heresy. This led to a growing sense of discontent among the Protestant population, who yearned for religious freedom and the ability to practice their faith without fear of persecution.

The political situation in the Low Countries further exacerbated the conflict. The region was a collection of semi-autonomous provinces, each with its own traditions and interests. The provinces were ruled by various members of the Habsburg dynasty, including Margaret of Parma, the Duke of Alba, and the Duke of Parma. The centralization of power under King Philip II and his imposition of harsh measures deepened the divide between the local authorities and the central government.

In 1566, the Iconoclastic Fury, or the Beeldenstorm, erupted as a violent manifestation of religious tensions. Calvinist mobs and iconoclasts targeted Catholic churches and monasteries, vandalizing and destroying religious images and artifacts. This marked a turning point in the conflict and further polarized the Catholic and Protestant factions.

The Beeldenstorm was followed by the Compromise of Nobles in 1566, where a group of Protestant and Catholic nobles petitioned the governor, Margaret of Parma, to ease religious restrictions. The petition sought to protect the rights of individual provinces and grant religious tolerance. While the petition was initially met with a degree of leniency, King Philip II soon rejected it and dispatched the Duke of Alba to suppress the rebellion.

The arrival of the Duke of Alba marked the beginning of a more intense and brutal phase of the conflict. Alba initiated a reign of terror, instituting the infamous Council of Troubles, known as the "Council of Blood," which ruthlessly pursued and executed suspected rebels and heretics. Thousands were put to death, and the atrocities committed during this period further inflamed the Dutch population.

The Dutch Revolt, fueled by a desire for religious freedom and resistance against Spanish tyranny, gained momentum. In 1568, the war officially began when William of Orange, also known as William the Silent, a leading nobleman and military commander, launched a series of campaigns against Spanish forces. Throughout the conflict, the Dutch rebels faced significant challenges, including a formidable Spanish army led by talented commanders such as the Duke of Parma. Battles like the Battle of Heiligerlee (1568), the

Siege of Leiden (1573-1574), and the Relief of Goes (1576) were pivotal moments in the war.

The conflict was not solely a religious struggle but also a political one. In 1581, the Act of Abjuration, also known as the Plakkaat van Verlatinghe, was signed by representatives of several northern provinces. This declaration of independence formally renounced allegiance to King Philip II, stating that a ruler who failed to protect the rights and liberties of the people could be deposed. It laid the groundwork for the eventual recognition of Dutch independence.

The international context of the Eighty Years' War also played a role. The Dutch rebels sought alliances and support from foreign powers, including England and France, to counter Spanish forces. The Treaty of Nonsuch (1585) between England and the Dutch rebels, signed by Queen Elizabeth I, provided much-needed financial and military aid to the Dutch cause.

The war continued for several more decades, marked by battles, sieges, and shifting alliances. The Treaty of Westphalia in 1648 formally recognized the independence of the Dutch Republic from Spanish rule, ending the Eighty Years' War. The Peace of Münster, a component of the Treaty of Westphalia, specifically acknowledged the sovereignty of the Dutch Republic and its right to practice its own religion.

The birth of Dutch independence was a complex and protracted process, driven by religious, political, and economic factors. It marked the emergence of the Dutch Republic as a unique and influential European nation. The legacy of the Eighty Years' War endures in the Dutch national identity, with the struggle for freedom and tolerance remaining integral to the Dutch ethos.

The Dutch East India Company (VOC): A Global Trading Power

The Dutch East India Company, known by its Dutch acronym VOC (Verenigde Oost-Indische Compagnie), stands as a testament to the economic prowess and maritime dominance of the Dutch Republic during the Age of Exploration and Colonialism. Established in 1602, the VOC would become one of the world's first multinational corporations and a key player in the global spice trade, leaving an indelible mark on world history.

The VOC's formation was a response to the burgeoning trade opportunities in the East Indies, present-day Indonesia, which were abundant in valuable spices such as cloves, nutmeg, and pepper. Recognizing the immense potential for profit, Dutch merchants and investors came together to create a joint-stock company that would revolutionize the way trade was conducted.

Under the leadership of the VOC, the Dutch Republic established a monopoly over the spice trade in the East Indies, with a particular focus on the Moluccas, known as the "Spice Islands." This monopoly was enforced through a combination of military might and intricate trade agreements with indigenous rulers. The VOC maintained a formidable fleet and a standing army, ensuring that its interests were protected and its dominance unchallenged.

The VOC's operations extended far beyond the spice trade. The company conducted a wide range of activities, including trading in textiles, porcelain, precious metals, and various exotic goods. It established trading posts, forts, and settlements throughout Asia, from the Cape of Good Hope in South Africa to the shores of Japan. The VOC's network of fortified outposts and factories enabled it to control trade routes and access valuable resources.

One of the most iconic aspects of the VOC's legacy is its role in the global exploration and mapping of the world. The company sponsored numerous voyages of discovery, with explorers like Abel Tasman and Willem Janszoon making significant contributions to the mapping of Australia and New Zealand. Tasman's voyages, in particular, expanded the known world and opened up new possibilities for trade and colonization.

The VOC's success was built on innovative business practices, including the issuance of shares to investors, the creation of a standardized currency (the Dutch rijksdaalder), and the development of a corporate governance structure that included a board of directors and executive officers. These practices laid the foundation for modern corporate governance and are still studied by economists and business scholars today.

The Dutch East India Company was also responsible for introducing many new products and ideas to Europe. The trade between Asia and Europe, often referred to as the "Columbian Exchange," brought exotic spices, textiles, porcelain, tea, and coffee to the Western world. These goods not only transformed European cuisine but also had a profound impact on culture, fashion, and daily life.

The VOC's influence extended to the political landscape of Southeast Asia. The company's control over trade routes and territories allowed it to exert considerable influence over local rulers and states. In some cases, the VOC effectively functioned as a de facto colonial power, establishing its own governments and enforcing its rules and regulations.

However, the VOC's dominance and ambition were not without controversy and conflict. The company's monopoly and aggressive tactics often led to tensions with other European colonial powers, particularly the Portuguese, English, and Spanish. The competition for dominance in the spice trade led to naval battles and conflicts in the Indian Ocean and Southeast Asia.

The VOC's profitability was not sustained indefinitely. Over time, the costs of maintaining its vast trading network and military apparatus began to strain its financial resources. Corruption and mismanagement within the company also took a toll on its profitability. By the late 18th century, the VOC was burdened by debt and struggling to maintain control over its vast territories.

In 1799, the VOC was officially dissolved, marking the end of an era. Its assets and territories were transferred to the Dutch government, and the company's archives provide a valuable historical record of its operations and the early years of global trade.

Despite its eventual decline and dissolution, the VOC's impact on the world cannot be overstated. It laid the groundwork for modern multinational corporations, shaped global trade routes, contributed to the development of capitalism, and introduced European society to the richness of Asian culture and goods.

The Dutch Golden Age: Art, Science, and Commerce

The Dutch Golden Age, a period of unparalleled prosperity and cultural flourishing in the 17th century, stands as one of the most remarkable chapters in Dutch history. This era, often referred to as the "Golden Century," saw the Dutch Republic ascend to global prominence as a center of trade, art, science, and innovation.

At the heart of the Dutch Golden Age was the Dutch Republic's emergence as a global economic powerhouse. The country's strategic location, with access to both the Atlantic and the Baltic, made it a hub for international trade. Dutch merchants and shipbuilders constructed a vast fleet of ships that dominated global commerce, establishing the Dutch Republic as a formidable maritime trading nation.

The Dutch East India Company (VOC) and the Dutch West India Company (WIC) played pivotal roles in expanding Dutch trade networks. The VOC, as previously discussed, controlled the spice trade in the East Indies, while the WIC was involved in the transatlantic slave trade and the colonization of the Americas. These companies, with their vast resources and global reach, contributed significantly to the Dutch Republic's economic success.

The Dutch Golden Age was marked by a culture of entrepreneurship and innovation. Dutch merchants and traders developed sophisticated financial instruments, including the Amsterdam Stock Exchange, which became one of the world's first stock markets. This financial innovation laid the groundwork for modern capitalism and investment practices.

Dutch cities, most notably Amsterdam, flourished as centers of commerce and finance. The city's famous canals, designed for both transportation and defense, became bustling hubs of economic activity. The Amsterdam Exchange Bank, established in 1609, introduced the concept of banknotes and provided a stable currency for trade.

The Dutch Republic's prosperity extended to its art and culture. The Dutch Golden Age produced a remarkable array of artistic talent, with painters, poets, writers, and scientists making significant contributions to the world's cultural heritage.

Dutch painting, in particular, reached its zenith during this period. The Dutch Masters, including Rembrandt van Rijn, Johannes Vermeer, and Frans Hals, produced masterpieces that are celebrated to this day. Rembrandt's evocative use of light and shadow, Vermeer's exquisite genre scenes, and Hals' lively portraits are just a few examples of the artistic brilliance that defined this era.

The subject matter of Dutch paintings was diverse, ranging from landscapes and still lifes to scenes of everyday life and portraits. Artists captured the vibrant tapestry of Dutch society, reflecting the wealth, diversity, and burgeoning middle class of the Republic.

Literature also thrived during the Dutch Golden Age. The works of Joost van den Vondel, considered the greatest Dutch playwright and poet of the era, continue to be celebrated for their literary excellence and moral depth. His epic drama "Gijsbrecht van Aemstel" and his poems on religious themes remain enduring classics.

Scientific progress was another hallmark of the Dutch Golden Age. The Dutch Republic was home to pioneering scientists like Antonie van Leeuwenhoek, who made groundbreaking discoveries in microbiology, and Christiaan Huygens, known for his work in optics and mechanics. Huygens also invented the pendulum clock, a technological advancement that revolutionized timekeeping.

The Dutch commitment to education and intellectual pursuits was evident in the establishment of Leiden University in 1575, one of the oldest universities in the Netherlands. The university played a vital role in fostering scholarship and scientific inquiry.

The Dutch Golden Age was not without its challenges. The Republic's economic success drew envy and competition from other European powers. Wars, such as the Eighty Years' War and the Anglo-Dutch Wars, tested the Dutch Republic's resilience. However, its formidable navy and strategic prowess allowed it to maintain its status as a major power.

The decline of the Dutch Golden Age came gradually, as economic shifts and military conflicts took their toll. The Treaty of Utrecht in 1713 marked the end of the Republic's dominance in world trade, and the era's cultural and artistic legacy began to wane.

Nevertheless, the Dutch Golden Age remains an enduring symbol of a nation's extraordinary achievements in art, science, commerce, and culture. Its legacy continues to inspire and captivate, reminding us of the profound impact that a small, dynamic republic could have on the world stage.

Dutch Exploration and Colonization

The Dutch Republic's role in the Age of Exploration and Colonization is a testament to the country's maritime prowess, commercial ambitions, and global reach during the 17th century. While often overshadowed by other colonial powers like Spain, Portugal, and England, the Dutch made significant contributions to the expansion of the known world, leaving an enduring legacy in various parts of the globe.

Dutch exploration was driven by a desire for new trade routes and markets. The Dutch Republic's strategic location on the coast of the North Sea and its burgeoning middle class of merchants and traders laid the foundation for a maritime empire. Dutch ships, renowned for their speed and efficiency, became a common sight on the seas as Dutch explorers set out to chart uncharted territories and establish new trade networks.

One of the notable Dutch explorers of this era was Abel Tasman. In 1642, Tasman embarked on a groundbreaking voyage sponsored by the Dutch East India Company (VOC). His journey took him to the vast waters of the South Pacific, where he became one of the first Europeans to discover and map Tasmania and New Zealand. Tasman's voyages opened up new possibilities for trade and colonization in the region.

Another significant Dutch explorer was Willem Janszoon, who in 1606, became the first European to set foot on the Australian continent. Janszoon's landing on the northern coast of Australia marked the beginning of European exploration and interest in the continent, which would later lead to Dutch and British colonization.

The Dutch Republic's colonization efforts extended to the Americas as well. The Dutch West India Company (WIC) played a prominent role in establishing Dutch colonies in the New World. In 1624, the Dutch established New Amsterdam on the southern tip of Manhattan Island, now known as New York City. This settlement became a thriving Dutch trading post and a hub for the fur trade.

The Dutch also laid claim to other parts of the Americas, including the Caribbean islands of Aruba, Bonaire, and Curaçao, as well as parts of present-day Brazil. These colonies were valued for their agricultural production and strategic locations along trade routes.

In South Asia, the Dutch established a strong presence in the Indonesian archipelago, which was rich in spices such as cloves, nutmeg, and pepper. The VOC played a central role in Dutch efforts to control the spice trade in the East Indies. The Dutch Republic's dominance in this region not only fueled its economic prosperity but also led to the establishment of colonial outposts and forts across the Indonesian archipelago.

In Africa, the Dutch established the Cape Colony at the southern tip of the continent in 1652. This settlement, initially a refreshment station for VOC ships, would later become a Dutch colony known as the Cape of Good Hope. The colony's strategic location on the maritime route to the Dutch East Indies made it a valuable asset for the Dutch Republic.

Dutch exploration and colonization were characterized by a pragmatic and profit-driven approach. The Dutch sought to establish trading posts, fortifications, and colonies where they could access valuable resources, maintain control over trade routes, and generate profits. Religious motivations, often a driving force in colonization for other European powers, played a lesser role in Dutch expansion.

The Dutch Republic's global reach was also marked by its commitment to free trade and religious tolerance. Dutch colonies were known for their relatively inclusive policies toward different religious and ethnic groups, creating a diverse and cosmopolitan atmosphere in many of these settlements.

As the Dutch Republic rose to prominence as a colonial power, it faced competition and conflicts with other European nations, particularly England and France. The Anglo-Dutch Wars of the 17th century, for example, were a series of naval conflicts that underscored the rivalry between England and the Dutch Republic for control over trade routes and colonial territories.

The Dutch Republic's colonial empire, while extensive, was not without its challenges and eventual decline. Economic shifts, military conflicts, and changing geopolitical dynamics in the 18th century would gradually erode Dutch colonial power.

Tulip Mania: The Peculiar Dutch Obsession

Tulip Mania, one of the most intriguing episodes in financial history, unfolded in the Dutch Republic during the 17th century. This peculiar phenomenon marked a period of frenzied speculation and skyrocketing prices for tulip bulbs, ultimately culminating in a speculative bubble and a spectacular economic crash.

The origins of Tulip Mania can be traced back to the introduction of tulips to Europe from the Ottoman Empire in the late 16th century. These vibrant and exotic flowers, with their intricate and striking patterns, quickly captivated the Dutch elite and became a symbol of wealth and status. The tulip's popularity grew, and Dutch horticulturists began to cultivate and hybridize new varieties, leading to a wide array of colors and shapes.

By the early 17th century, tulips had become a highly sought-after commodity, with bulbs fetching ever-increasing prices in the Dutch Republic. This fascination with tulips coincided with the Dutch Republic's rise as an economic powerhouse, fueled by trade, commerce, and a burgeoning middle class. As a result, the Dutch Republic had a thriving culture of conspicuous consumption, and tulips became a conspicuous symbol of this newfound affluence.

Tulip Mania took off in earnest during the 1630s. Prices for rare tulip bulbs began to soar, driven by a speculative fervor that saw bulbs changing hands multiple times in a single day. The tulip market developed into a complex and speculative financial system, with options and futures contracts trading on the future prices of bulbs.

One of the most coveted tulip varieties during the height of Tulip Mania was the Semper Augustus. This particular tulip had a striking red and white striped pattern, making it one of the most sought-after flowers of its time. The prices for Semper Augustus bulbs reached astronomical levels, with some bulbs reportedly selling for the equivalent of a luxurious canal-side house in Amsterdam.

The frenzy reached its zenith in early 1637 when the price of tulip bulbs, particularly rare and exotic varieties, reached absurd levels. The tulip market had become an unsustainable bubble, with investors and speculators driving up prices to unsustainable heights. The speculative fever had spread far and wide, involving individuals from all walks of life, from wealthy merchants to common artisans.

However, the bubble was destined to burst. In February 1637, the market suddenly collapsed. Prices plummeted, leaving many investors with worthless tulip contracts and bulbs that were now worth a fraction of their previous value. The sudden and dramatic crash of Tulip Mania resulted in significant financial losses and ruined many who had invested heavily in the market.

In the aftermath of the crash, the Dutch government attempted to regulate and stabilize the tulip trade. Some traders and speculators who had been left holding worthless contracts were given lenient terms to settle their debts, while others faced legal action.

Tulip Mania is often cited as one of the earliest recorded speculative bubbles in history. It serves as a cautionary tale of the dangers of irrational exuberance and the consequences of unchecked speculation. While it did not lead to a broader economic crisis in the Dutch Republic, it did expose the risks associated with speculative trading and the potential for market manipulation.

Despite the financial disaster that Tulip Mania brought to many, the Dutch fascination with tulips endured. Tulips continued to be cultivated and admired, and the Netherlands remains renowned for its stunning tulip fields and the annual Keukenhof Gardens, a testament to the enduring appeal of these beautiful flowers.

In retrospect, Tulip Mania represents a peculiar chapter in Dutch history, a time when the allure of a single flower led to a speculative frenzy that captured the imagination of a nation and, briefly, the financial world. It stands as a curious reminder of the unpredictability of human behavior when it comes to matters of wealth and desire.

The Dutch Republic: A Model of Republicanism

The Dutch Republic, often referred to simply as the "Republic of the Seven United Netherlands," emerged as a unique and influential political entity during the 17th century. This period of Dutch history was characterized by the country's transformation into a republic and its distinctive republican form of government, which stood as a model of political innovation and tolerance.

The Dutch Republic's journey towards republicanism was shaped by a complex interplay of historical, political, and religious factors. In the late 16th century, the Dutch provinces that would eventually form the republic were part of the larger Spanish Habsburg Empire. However, as the Protestant Reformation swept through Europe, religious tensions and conflicts began to emerge in the Low Countries.

One of the pivotal events that set the stage for the Dutch Republic's birth was the Eighty Years' War (also known as the Dutch War of Independence) against Spanish rule. This protracted and bloody conflict, which spanned from 1568 to 1648, was marked by a struggle for religious freedom and political autonomy. The Dutch rebels, led by figures like William of Orange, sought to break free from the rule of King Philip II of Spain, who was staunchly Catholic and sought to suppress Protestantism.

The Eighty Years' War saw the emergence of a decentralized and federalist structure within the Dutch provinces. The Union of Utrecht in 1579 brought several northern provinces together in a formal alliance, laying the groundwork for the future Dutch Republic. In 1581, the Act of Abjuration (Plakkaat van Verlatinghe) formalized the rejection of Philip II's authority and declared that rulers could be deposed if they failed to protect the rights and liberties of their subjects.

In 1588, the northern provinces officially declared their independence from Spain and established the Dutch Republic. This act marked a significant departure from the prevailing monarchies and empires of the time, as the Dutch Republic became one of the few republican states in early modern Europe.

The political structure of the Dutch Republic was unique and innovative. The country was a confederation of seven semi-autonomous provinces: Holland, Zeeland, Utrecht, Gelderland, Overijssel, Friesland, and Groningen. Each province had its own government and enjoyed a degree of sovereignty. The absence of a centralized monarchy led to a system of government characterized by federalism and checks and balances.

One of the defining features of the Dutch Republic's political system was its commitment to religious tolerance. The Republic became a safe haven for religious dissenters and minority groups fleeing persecution elsewhere in Europe. Jews, Huguenots, and various sects of Protestantism found refuge in the Dutch Republic, contributing to its cultural and intellectual diversity.

The Dutch Republic's republican government was characterized by a system of "regents" or city rulers who governed on behalf of the urban bourgeoisie. Cities like Amsterdam, Rotterdam, and The Hague were centers of political power and economic influence. The regents played a significant role in shaping the policies of the Republic.

Economically, the Dutch Republic prospered during this period. It became a global economic powerhouse, with a dominant position in trade, shipping, and finance. The Dutch East India Company (VOC) and the Dutch West India Company (WIC) were instrumental in expanding Dutch trade networks and establishing colonies overseas.

The Dutch Republic's republican form of government was influential and served as a model for later republican movements and political thought. The writings of Dutch philosopher Hugo Grotius, known for his work on international law, had a profound impact on the development of political theory and the concept of natural rights.

Despite its remarkable achievements, the Dutch Republic faced its own challenges and internal divisions. Political rivalries between the provinces, conflicts with neighboring European powers, and economic fluctuations tested the resilience of the Republic.

The Dutch Republic's republican experiment lasted for nearly two centuries, until it was replaced by the Kingdom of Holland under Napoleon Bonaparte's rule in 1806. Nevertheless, the legacy of the Dutch Republic endures in the principles of tolerance, federalism, and republicanism that it championed. It remains a model of republican governance and political innovation in the annals of history, embodying the spirit of freedom, diversity, and pragmatism that characterized this remarkable period in Dutch history.

The Anglo-Dutch Wars: Maritime Supremacy

The Anglo-Dutch Wars, a series of three conflicts that erupted in the 17th century between the English and Dutch naval powers, were pivotal events in the struggle for maritime supremacy and global dominance. These wars, which took place from 1652 to 1674, marked a significant chapter in the history of naval warfare and had far-reaching implications for the balance of power in Europe and beyond.

The origins of the Anglo-Dutch Wars can be traced back to a complex web of political, economic, and territorial disputes. At the heart of these conflicts lay the competition for control over trade routes, colonies, and valuable overseas possessions. The English, led by Oliver Cromwell's Commonwealth and later by Charles II, sought to challenge the Dutch Republic's dominance in global trade and navigation.

The First Anglo-Dutch War (1652-1654) was characterized by a series of naval engagements between the English and Dutch fleets. The English, under the leadership of General-at-Sea Robert Blake, sought to curtail Dutch trade and break the Dutch monopoly over important commodities such as spices and textiles. The war culminated in the Treaty of Westminster in 1654, which temporarily ended hostilities but did not fully resolve the underlying issues.

The respite provided by the Treaty of Westminster was short-lived, as the Second Anglo-Dutch War (1665-1667) erupted over disputes related to trade, colonial possessions, and territorial boundaries. This conflict witnessed some of the largest and bloodiest naval battles of the age, including the Battle of Lowestoft in 1665 and the Four Days' Battle in

1666. The Dutch, under Admiral Michiel de Ruyter, demonstrated their formidable naval prowess, but the war ultimately concluded with the Treaty of Breda in 1667, which restored some territorial possessions but left many issues unresolved.

The Third Anglo-Dutch War (1672-1674), also known as the Dutch War or the Franco-Dutch War, was the final installment in this series of conflicts. This war saw the Dutch Republic pitted against a coalition of England, France, and several other European powers. The English, now under the reign of Charles II, joined forces with France against the Dutch in an attempt to break Dutch commercial dominance. The war resulted in several significant naval battles, including the Battle of Solebay in 1672. The Treaty of Westminster in 1674 brought an end to the hostilities.

Throughout the Anglo-Dutch Wars, both sides demonstrated remarkable naval innovations and tactics. The English developed the "line of battle," a formation that allowed them to concentrate firepower on the enemy, while the Dutch introduced advancements such as the "zeilend oorlogsschip" or "ship of the line," which influenced the design of future warships.

The legacy of the Anglo-Dutch Wars was multifaceted. While no clear victor emerged from these conflicts, the Dutch Republic maintained its status as a global trading power. The wars also laid the groundwork for the emergence of the Royal Navy as a dominant naval force in the following century.

The treaties that concluded each war reshaped colonial possessions and trade networks. The Treaty of Breda, for example, saw the English gain control of New Amsterdam, which was subsequently renamed New York, while the

Dutch retained their hold on the valuable Spice Islands in the East Indies.

The Anglo-Dutch Wars had broader implications for European geopolitics. The Dutch Republic's ability to hold its own against powerful adversaries like England and France highlighted its resilience and the effectiveness of its naval forces. These conflicts contributed to the eventual decline of the Dutch Republic as a global power, but they also underscored the importance of naval supremacy in shaping the course of history.

In conclusion, the Anglo-Dutch Wars were pivotal in the struggle for maritime supremacy and influence during the 17th century. These conflicts showcased the naval prowess of both the English and Dutch and had lasting effects on trade, colonial possessions, and the balance of power in Europe.

The Glorious Revolution and William of Orange

The Glorious Revolution of 1688 was a watershed moment in English history, marking a significant turning point in the country's constitutional and political development. At the heart of this transformative event was the Dutch prince, William of Orange, who played a central role in shaping the course of events.

William of Orange, also known as William III, Prince of Orange, was born on November 4, 1650, in The Hague, in what is now the Netherlands. He was a member of the House of Orange-Nassau, a prominent European dynasty. William's family had a history of resistance against the absolute power of the Spanish Habsburgs, which had ruled the Dutch Republic and its territories for much of the 16th and 17th centuries.

William's early life was marked by the ongoing struggle for Dutch independence from Spanish rule. He was educated in matters of statecraft, military strategy, and diplomacy, as his family prepared him for the role he would later play in the affairs of Europe. His training in governance and leadership would prove invaluable in the years to come.

In 1672, at the age of 21, William married his cousin, Mary Stuart, the daughter of the future King James II of England. This marriage was not merely a union of love but also a strategic alliance, as it solidified William's connections within European royalty and his role in continental politics.

The political landscape in England was complex at the time. King James II, a Roman Catholic, was determined to promote Catholicism in a predominantly Protestant nation. His attempts to grant religious freedom to Catholics and undermine the authority of the Anglican Church created deep-seated resentment among the Protestant majority.

As concerns grew about the potential establishment of a Catholic dynasty, leading English political figures, both Whigs and Tories, sought a solution to safeguard Protestantism and constitutional liberties. They looked to William of Orange as a possible savior of the Protestant cause and invited him to intervene in English affairs.

In November 1688, William and his fleet, known as the "Glorious Army," landed in the southwest of England, an event that would become known as the Glorious Revolution. William's arrival was met with a largely positive response from many influential figures in England, including Protestant nobles and members of Parliament.

King James II faced a crisis of confidence as support for William grew. Fearing for his safety and the stability of his reign, James fled England in December 1688. This abdication marked a bloodless transition of power, a remarkable departure from previous episodes of political upheaval.

The Convention Parliament, convened in January 1689, declared that James had effectively abdicated by fleeing the country and that the throne was vacant. In their Declaration of Right, Parliament outlined a series of grievances against James's rule, asserting that his policies and actions had violated the rights and liberties of English subjects.

In February 1689, William and Mary were jointly offered the English throne as constitutional monarchs, with certain conditions. They accepted the offer and were crowned as co-monarchs, William III and Mary II. This event marked the beginning of the joint reign of the new monarchs and the establishment of the constitutional monarchy that would come to define England.

The Glorious Revolution had profound implications for the development of English constitutionalism. It resulted in the promulgation of the Bill of Rights in 1689, which affirmed parliamentary supremacy, limited the powers of the monarchy, and protected the rights of subjects. This document laid the foundation for the modern British constitutional monarchy.

William III's reign was characterized by his commitment to defending Protestantism and upholding the constitutional principles enshrined in the Bill of Rights. He faced challenges, including the Williamite War in Ireland, where he sought to suppress Catholic Jacobite forces loyal to James II. The Battle of the Boyne in 1690, which resulted in a decisive victory for William, solidified his position in Ireland.

In Europe, William of Orange played a central role in the Grand Alliance, a coalition of European powers formed to oppose the expansionist ambitions of Louis XIV of France. The Nine Years' War (also known as the War of the League of Augsburg) saw William lead the coalition against France. The war ended with the Treaty of Ryswick in 1697, which preserved the balance of power in Europe.

Tragically, William's life was cut short when he died in a riding accident on March 8, 1702. His death marked the end of the Stuart dynasty's rule in England, as Mary II had preceded him in death, and the English throne passed to Mary's sister, Anne.

William of Orange's legacy endures as a pivotal figure in the history of England and the broader European context. His role in the Glorious Revolution and his commitment to constitutional government left an indelible mark on the development of parliamentary democracy in England. His influence extended far beyond his lifetime, shaping the foundations of the constitutional monarchy that prevails in the United Kingdom to this day. William of Orange's enduring legacy lies in his pivotal role in establishing the principles of constitutionalism, religious tolerance, and political liberty that continue to define modern democratic societies.

The Dutch Empire: Global Expansion

The Dutch Empire, also known as the Dutch Colonial Empire, was a vast and influential overseas empire that emerged during the Age of Exploration and reached its zenith during the 17th century. The Dutch Republic, a small and relatively young nation, became a major player on the global stage through a combination of maritime expertise, trade acumen, and a pragmatic approach to colonialism.

The early seeds of the Dutch Empire were sown in the late 16th century when Dutch explorers and traders set their sights on distant lands. The Dutch Republic's strategic location along the North Sea coast and its thriving middle class of merchants and traders provided the ideal foundation for maritime expansion. Key elements of the Dutch Empire's global reach included exploration, trade, and the establishment of colonies and trading posts in strategic locations.

One of the most notable institutions of Dutch colonial expansion was the Dutch East India Company (VOC), founded in 1602. The VOC was a joint-stock company granted a government-backed monopoly on Dutch trade in the East Indies, which included the present-day Indonesian archipelago. The VOC's mission was to dominate the spice trade, particularly cloves, nutmeg, and pepper, which were highly sought-after commodities in Europe.

The VOC's success in the East Indies was extraordinary. It established a vast network of trading posts, fortified settlements, and factories throughout the Indonesian archipelago. The Dutch controlled the production and distribution of spices, transforming them into valuable commodities that would shape global trade for centuries.

In the Americas, the Dutch West India Company (WIC), established in 1621, played a significant role in Dutch colonial expansion. The WIC focused on the Atlantic world, including the Caribbean and parts of South America. Dutch colonies in the Americas, such as New Amsterdam (later renamed New York) and the Dutch Caribbean islands of Aruba, Bonaire, and Curaçao, became important centers of trade, agriculture, and commerce.

The Dutch Republic's global reach extended to Africa, where it established forts and trading posts along the west coast. The Cape Colony, founded in 1652 at the southern tip of Africa, served as a refreshment station for VOC ships en route to the East Indies, eventually evolving into a Dutch colony known as the Cape of Good Hope.

Trade was the lifeblood of the Dutch Empire. Dutch merchant ships sailed to all corners of the globe, trading not only in spices but also in a wide range of goods, including textiles, ceramics, and precious metals. Dutch merchants and sailors ventured to Asia, Africa, the Americas, and even the Arctic, establishing an extensive web of trade routes and commercial networks.

The Dutch Empire's approach to colonialism differed from that of other European powers of the time. Rather than imposing strict control over their colonies, the Dutch often entered into mutually beneficial relationships with local rulers and indigenous peoples. This pragmatic approach allowed for the coexistence of diverse cultures within Dutch colonial territories, fostering tolerance and diversity.

Religious tolerance was another hallmark of Dutch colonialism. Unlike some other European colonial powers, the Dutch Republic did not enforce religious conformity in its colonies. This policy attracted religious dissenters and minority groups, contributing to a cosmopolitan atmosphere in many Dutch colonial settlements.

The Dutch Empire's global expansion brought both economic prosperity and geopolitical challenges. It faced competition and conflicts with other European nations, including England and France. The Anglo-Dutch Wars of the 17th century, for example, were a series of naval conflicts that underscored the rivalry between England and the Dutch Republic for control over trade routes and colonial territories.

Despite its remarkable achievements, the Dutch Empire eventually began to decline in the late 17th century. Economic shifts, military conflicts, and changing geopolitical dynamics took their toll on Dutch colonial power. The English successfully seized control of New Amsterdam in 1664, renaming it New York, while the French expanded their influence in the Caribbean.

By the 18th century, the Dutch Empire had ceded much of its colonial territories to other European powers. However, its legacy endured in the form of cultural exchanges, economic ties, and the enduring Dutch presence in regions like Indonesia, Suriname, and the Caribbean.

In conclusion, the Dutch Empire's global expansion during the Age of Exploration and the 17th century was marked by its maritime expertise, trade dominance, and pragmatic approach to colonialism. The Dutch Republic's legacy lives on in the cultural, economic, and historical connections it forged with regions across the world.

Rembrandt and Dutch Baroque Art

The Dutch Golden Age, a period of remarkable cultural and economic growth in the 17th century Netherlands, gave rise to a flourishing of artistic creativity. At the forefront of this artistic renaissance was Rembrandt Harmenszoon van Rijn, one of the most celebrated painters in the history of art. Rembrandt's innovative and deeply emotive works exemplify the essence of Dutch Baroque art, a style characterized by intricate detail, vivid realism, and a profound exploration of the human condition.

Rembrandt was born in Leiden, the Netherlands, on July 15, 1606. He demonstrated an early aptitude for art and began his formal training under the renowned history painter Jacob van Swanenburgh. Later, he moved to Amsterdam, where he apprenticed with Pieter Lastman, a painter known for his biblical and historical scenes. Rembrandt's exposure to these diverse artistic influences laid the foundation for his distinctive style.

The hallmark of Rembrandt's art was his ability to capture the play of light and shadow, a technique known as chiaroscuro. This mastery of light and dark not only lent depth and dimension to his paintings but also allowed him to explore the subtleties of human expression and emotion. Rembrandt's use of chiaroscuro is particularly evident in his portraits, where he skillfully illuminated his subjects' faces, revealing their inner thoughts and personalities.

One of Rembrandt's most iconic works, "The Night Watch" (1642), showcases his exceptional talent. This monumental group portrait of a civic militia, originally known as the "Militia Company of District II under the Command of Captain Frans Banninck Cocq," is a testament to Rembrandt's ability to infuse a seemingly ordinary scene with drama, vitality, and psychological depth. The dynamic composition, the play of light on the characters, and the intense expressions of the figures make it a masterpiece of Dutch Baroque art.

In addition to portraiture, Rembrandt's oeuvre encompassed a wide range of subjects, including biblical narratives, historical scenes, landscapes, and etchings. His biblical works, such as "The Return of the Prodigal Son" (1669) and "The Jewish Bride" (c. 1667), are renowned for their spiritual depth and emotional resonance. Rembrandt's ability to convey the humanity of his subjects, even in sacred contexts, set his work apart from his contemporaries.

Rembrandt's technique extended to his etchings and printmaking. His etchings, such as "The Three Crosses" (1653), demonstrate his skill in creating intricate, detailed compositions with a rich interplay of light and shadow. These works allowed him to reach a wider audience and further cemented his reputation as a master of the medium.

While Rembrandt's artistic brilliance is celebrated today, his personal life was marked by financial challenges and personal tragedies. Despite his success as a painter, Rembrandt faced financial difficulties due to his lavish lifestyle and business ventures. In 1656, he declared bankruptcy, and his possessions, including his art collection and house, were auctioned off.

Tragedy also touched Rembrandt's personal life. His beloved wife, Saskia van Uylenburgh, with whom he had four children, passed away in 1642. Rembrandt's second marriage to Hendrickje Stoffels, his housemaid, scandalized society but provided him with companionship and support.

In the later years of his life, Rembrandt's style evolved, becoming more introspective and reflective. His self-portraits from this period are particularly poignant, revealing the toll of age and life's hardships on the artist. The introspective quality of these works adds to their emotional depth and complexity.

Rembrandt passed away on October 4, 1669, in Amsterdam. His legacy endures not only in his body of work but also in the profound influence he had on subsequent generations of artists. His innovative techniques, his exploration of light and shadow, and his ability to capture the human soul continue to inspire and captivate art lovers and scholars worldwide.

Dutch Baroque art, epitomized by Rembrandt's genius, remains a testament to the creative brilliance of the Dutch Golden Age. Its impact on the art world and the enduring fascination with Rembrandt's work serve as a testament to the enduring power of his artistry and the timeless appeal of Dutch Baroque aesthetics.

The Scientific Revolution in the Netherlands

The Scientific Revolution, a transformative period in the history of science, was marked by profound changes in the way humans understood the natural world. While often associated with figures like Copernicus, Galileo, and Newton, the Scientific Revolution had a significant impact in the Netherlands as well, contributing to advancements in various fields of science.

During the 17th century, the Dutch Republic was at the forefront of scientific inquiry and innovation. The reasons for the Dutch Republic's prominence in the Scientific Revolution can be attributed to several key factors. Firstly, the Dutch Republic was a thriving center of trade and commerce, which fostered a culture of curiosity and openness to new ideas from different parts of the world. Secondly, it was a nation characterized by religious and political tolerance, providing an environment where scholars and scientists could pursue their research without fear of persecution. Finally, the Dutch had a strong tradition of practical, hands-on knowledge, which was conducive to scientific experimentation.

One of the most notable figures in the Dutch Scientific Revolution was Antonie van Leeuwenhoek (1632-1723), a self-taught scientist and microscopist. Van Leeuwenhoek is often referred to as the "Father of Microbiology" for his pioneering work in microscopy. Using his handmade microscopes, he made remarkable discoveries about the microscopic world, including the first observations of bacteria, protozoa, and sperm cells. His meticulous observations and detailed letters to the Royal Society in London contributed significantly to the understanding of life at the microscopic level.

Another Dutch luminary of the Scientific Revolution was Christiaan Huygens (1629-1695), a polymath who made significant contributions to mathematics, physics, and astronomy. Huygens is best known for his work on the theory of light and his development of the wave theory of light propagation. He also constructed improved telescopes, enabling him to make detailed observations of celestial bodies. Huygens discovered Saturn's largest moon, Titan, and accurately described its ring system. His achievements in optics and astronomy had a profound impact on the field of optics and laid the groundwork for future discoveries in astronomy.

The Dutch Republic also played a role in the development of the scientific method, which became a cornerstone of modern science. Francis Bacon's ideas on empirical observation and induction, which laid the foundation for the scientific method, found fertile ground among Dutch scholars and scientists. This emphasis on systematic observation, experimentation, and the collection of data for analysis contributed to the advancement of various scientific disciplines.

Mathematics and cartography were areas in which Dutch scholars made significant contributions during the Scientific Revolution. Adriaan Metius, Willebrord Snellius, and Simon Stevin were among the mathematicians who made important strides in trigonometry and the measurement of angles. Stevin, in particular, introduced the decimal system to Europe, simplifying mathematical calculations. In cartography, Willem Blaeu and Joan Blaeu, a father-and-son team of mapmakers, produced some of the most accurate and detailed maps of the time, contributing to the advancement of navigation and exploration.

Medical science also saw progress in the Dutch Republic during this period. Herman Boerhaave, a physician and chemist, made significant contributions to the understanding of physiology and the classification of diseases. His work laid the foundation for modern medical education and the practice of clinical medicine.

The Dutch Scientific Revolution was not confined to a single field but encompassed a wide range of disciplines, including botany, chemistry, and mechanics. It was a testament to the spirit of inquiry, intellectual curiosity, and openness to new ideas that prevailed in the Dutch Republic during the 17th century. The contributions of Dutch scientists and scholars during this period continue to be celebrated and studied, reflecting their enduring impact on the world of science and knowledge.

In conclusion, the Scientific Revolution in the Netherlands during the 17th century was a vibrant and intellectually fertile period characterized by groundbreaking discoveries and advancements in various scientific disciplines. Figures like Antonie van Leeuwenhoek, Christiaan Huygens, and others made lasting contributions to fields ranging from microscopy and optics to mathematics and cartography.

Dutch Literature and Philosophy

The cultural effervescence of the Dutch Golden Age extended beyond the realms of art and science; it also gave rise to a flourishing tradition of literature and philosophy. This chapter explores the vibrant world of Dutch letters and thought during this remarkable period.

Dutch literature during the 17th century was characterized by a diversity of styles and genres, reflecting the dynamic society of the Dutch Republic. One of the notable figures in Dutch literature was Joost van den Vondel (1587-1679), often hailed as the "Prince of Dutch Poets." Vondel's prolific output spanned various forms, including plays, epic poetry, and lyrical verse. His historical dramas, such as "Gijsbrecht van Aemstel" (1637), celebrated Dutch history and identity, while his religious and moralistic works delved into profound philosophical themes.

Another luminary of Dutch literature was P.C. Hooft (1581-1647), a poet, playwright, and historian. Hooft's works embodied the ideals of the Dutch Renaissance, emphasizing humanism, classical learning, and civic virtue. His historical dramas, like "Granida" (1605) and "Geeraerdt van Velsen" (1613), offered insightful reflections on themes of love, honor, and duty.

The Dutch Republic was also home to renowned satirists and humorists. Jacob Cats (1577-1660), a prolific author, is known for his moralistic and didactic poetry. His emblem books, including "Sinne- en Minnebeelden" (1618), combined witty verses with symbolic illustrations, imparting moral lessons and wisdom. Cats' works appealed to a broad readership and contributed to the development of Dutch prose.

Philosophy found a fertile ground in the Dutch Republic during the Golden Age. One of the prominent philosophers of the era was René Descartes (1596-1650), a Frenchman who spent a significant portion of his life in the Dutch Republic. Descartes' groundbreaking work, "Meditations on First Philosophy" (1641), laid the foundation for modern philosophy by championing the use of reason and skepticism. His famous statement, "Cogito, ergo sum" ("I think, therefore I am"), encapsulated his commitment to doubt and critical thinking as the basis for knowledge.

Spinoza's philosophical ideas challenged prevailing religious and societal norms. His major work, "Ethics" (1677), explored questions of ethics, metaphysics, and the nature of God. Spinoza's concept of a pantheistic God and his call for religious tolerance positioned him as a controversial and influential thinker of his time.

In the realm of political philosophy, Hugo Grotius (1583-1645) made significant contributions. His work, "De jure belli ac pacis" ("On the Law of War and Peace," 1625), laid the groundwork for international law and the principles of just war. Grotius' ideas on natural law, the rights of individuals, and the sovereignty of states had a lasting impact on the development of international relations.

The Dutch Golden Age also witnessed the publication of one of the world's earliest newspapers, "Courante uyt Italien, Duytslandt, &c." (1620). This Dutch newspaper marked a significant development in the history of journalism, providing readers with timely news and information.

The flourishing of literature and philosophy in the Dutch Republic was supported by a growing literary market, a burgeoning printing industry, and a reading public eager for intellectual stimulation. The rise of coffeehouses and literary salons fostered a culture of discussion and exchange of ideas.

Dutch literature and philosophy of the Golden Age were deeply intertwined with the cultural, social, and political developments of the time. They reflected the spirit of inquiry, tolerance, and humanism that characterized Dutch society during this period. The legacy of these intellectual achievements endures, serving as a testament to the enduring influence of Dutch thought and literature on the broader European intellectual tradition.

Dutch Colonial Legacy: Indonesia and Beyond

The Dutch colonial legacy in Southeast Asia, particularly in Indonesia, is a complex and multifaceted chapter in the history of colonialism. The Dutch East India Company (VOC), established in 1602, played a pivotal role in shaping the colonial history of Indonesia and the broader region. This chapter delves into the enduring impact of Dutch colonial rule, its legacy, and the complexities it left behind.

The VOC, often considered the world's first multinational corporation, was granted a charter by the Dutch government to establish a monopoly over trade in the East Indies. This marked the beginning of Dutch involvement in the Indonesian archipelago, a vast and diverse region consisting of thousands of islands, cultures, and languages.

The primary objective of the VOC was to control the spice trade, particularly the production of cloves, nutmeg, and pepper, which were highly sought-after commodities in Europe. To achieve this, the VOC established a network of trading posts, fortified settlements, and factories across the Indonesian archipelago. The company's ruthless pursuit of profit often resulted in the exploitation of local resources and the imposition of a harsh and exploitative system of trade.

The Dutch colonial presence in Indonesia extended for nearly three centuries, and its legacy left an indelible mark on the region. The Dutch East Indies, as it came to be known, became a major source of wealth for the Dutch Republic and played a crucial role in financing the country's economic growth during the 17th century.

The impact of Dutch colonialism on Indonesia was profound and far-reaching. It influenced not only the economy but also the social, cultural, and political landscape of the region. The

Dutch introduced new agricultural practices, such as cash-crop cultivation, which transformed the Indonesian landscape and economy. They also played a role in shaping the administrative and legal systems of the colonies.

However, Dutch colonial rule was characterized by exploitative practices, forced labor, and the extraction of resources for the benefit of the Dutch East India Company and the Dutch government. Indigenous populations were subjected to harsh labor conditions on plantations, in mines, and in other industries.

The cultural legacy of Dutch colonialism in Indonesia is complex. While the Dutch introduced European customs, architecture, and Christianity, they also influenced Indonesian culture in ways that are still visible today. The Indonesian language, Bahasa Indonesia, incorporates many Dutch loanwords, reflecting the linguistic impact of colonialism. Additionally, elements of Dutch colonial architecture can still be seen in cities like Jakarta, formerly known as Batavia.

The legacy of Dutch colonialism in Indonesia is also marked by the struggle for independence. The period of Japanese occupation during World War II weakened Dutch colonial authority, and in 1945, Sukarno and Mohammad Hatta declared Indonesia's independence. This marked the beginning of a long and challenging struggle for independence, culminating in the recognition of Indonesia's sovereignty in 1949.

Beyond Indonesia, the Dutch colonial legacy extended to other parts of Southeast Asia. The Dutch controlled territories such as Suriname in South America and the Caribbean islands of Aruba, Bonaire, and Curaçao. In these regions, the legacy of Dutch colonialism is still evident in the language, culture, and legal systems.

Dutch in the Atlantic Slave Trade

The Atlantic Slave Trade, one of the darkest chapters in human history, involved the forced transportation of millions of Africans to the Americas as slaves. While it is often associated with European powers like Portugal, Spain, and Britain, the Dutch played a significant role in this brutal and inhumane trade.

The Dutch involvement in the Atlantic Slave Trade began in the early 17th century when they established a presence in the Americas and the Caribbean. The Dutch West India Company (WIC), chartered in 1621, was instrumental in this endeavor. The WIC's primary objectives were to establish colonies, trade, and exploit the resources of the Americas and West Africa.

The Dutch were actively engaged in the triangular trade, which involved the exchange of goods, enslaved Africans, and products such as sugar, tobacco, and cotton between Europe, Africa, and the Americas. Dutch traders would sail to West Africa, where they exchanged European goods, firearms, and alcohol for enslaved Africans. These captives were then transported across the Atlantic in horrendous conditions, often packed like sardines in the holds of ships during the Middle Passage.

The conditions on Dutch slave ships were deplorable, with countless Africans enduring unimaginable suffering and death. The mortality rate during the voyage was shockingly high, as slaves were subjected to overcrowding, disease, malnutrition, and violence. It is estimated that millions of Africans died during the Middle Passage as a result of these appalling conditions.

The enslaved Africans who survived the grueling journey were sold into forced labor on Dutch-owned plantations in the Americas, primarily in the Dutch colonies of Suriname, Curaçao, and New Netherland (later New York). These enslaved individuals toiled under brutal conditions, cultivating crops such as sugar, coffee, and indigo, which were highly profitable commodities for the Dutch.

The Dutch involvement in the Atlantic Slave Trade was not limited to transportation and labor; it extended to the financing and management of the trade as well. Dutch merchants, investors, and shipowners profited immensely from the trade in human beings. The economic gains made from the exploitation of enslaved Africans played a significant role in financing the Dutch economy during the 17th and 18th centuries.

The Dutch Atlantic slave trade continued for several centuries, with the Dutch being one of the last European powers to formally abolish the trade. In 1814, the Netherlands officially banned the slave trade, although it continued illegally for some time thereafter.

The legacy of Dutch involvement in the Atlantic Slave Trade is a painful one, marked by the suffering and dehumanization of millions of Africans. The effects of this trade on African diaspora communities in the Americas and the Caribbean are still felt today, as descendants of enslaved Africans continue to grapple with the historical trauma and systemic injustices stemming from this dark period.

The Napoleonic Era: Dutch Republic to Kingdom

The turn of the 19th century marked a significant transformation in the history of the Netherlands, as the country transitioned from a republic to a kingdom under the influence of the Napoleonic Empire. This period of change was characterized by political upheaval, territorial shifts, and the rise of Napoleon Bonaparte.

In 1795, French revolutionary forces, led by General Charles Pichegru, invaded the Dutch Republic, which was then known as the Batavian Republic. The Dutch Republic had been weakened by internal strife and external pressures, and it succumbed to French military might. As a result, the Batavian Republic was established as a client state of France, effectively ending the independent existence of the Dutch Republic.

The French influence on the Batavian Republic was significant, as it imposed several reforms and changes on the Dutch political landscape. The new government was modeled after the French revolutionary system, with a centralized administration and a strong executive branch. The Dutch legal system was reformed, and a new constitution was introduced, reflecting the principles of the French Revolution.

In 1806, Napoleon Bonaparte took a further step in reshaping the Dutch political landscape by installing his brother, Louis Bonaparte, as the King of Holland. This marked the transition from the Batavian Republic to the Kingdom of Holland. Louis Bonaparte ruled as a puppet monarch under the guidance of his brother, Napoleon. During his reign, he implemented various reforms,

81

including improvements in infrastructure, education, and the legal system.

One of the most enduring legacies of Louis Bonaparte's rule was his promotion of Dutch national identity and culture. He encouraged the use of the Dutch language and promoted Dutch art and literature. His reign also saw the publication of the first official Dutch national anthem, the "Wilhelmus."

However, Louis Bonaparte's reign was not without challenges. He often faced pressure from his brother, Napoleon, to prioritize French interests over Dutch ones. The economic blockade imposed by the British during the Napoleonic Wars further strained the Dutch economy.

In 1810, as part of Napoleon's Continental System, the French Empire annexed the Kingdom of Holland, incorporating it into the French Empire. This marked the end of Dutch independence once again. The Dutch territories were now directly governed by French officials, and the Dutch economy was subjected to the economic policies of the French Empire.

The period of French rule brought both benefits and hardships to the Dutch population. On one hand, it introduced modern administrative practices and legal reforms. On the other hand, it imposed heavy taxes and conscription for the French army, leading to discontent among the Dutch people.

The Napoleonic Era came to an end with the defeat of Napoleon at the Battle of Waterloo in 1815. The Congress of Vienna, which followed the defeat of Napoleon, sought to redraw the map of Europe and restore order to the continent. As part of this reorganization, the United Kingdom of the Netherlands was created in 1815, consisting of present-day Belgium and the Netherlands.

This union was intended to serve as a buffer state against French expansionism and to promote stability in the region.

The Napoleonic Era was a tumultuous period in Dutch history, marked by shifts in governance, political reforms, and challenges brought about by the French Empire. The transition from a republic to a kingdom and the subsequent formation of the United Kingdom of the Netherlands reflected the changing political dynamics of early 19th-century Europe and had a lasting impact on the nation's identity and political structure.

Independence Restored: The Kingdom of the Netherlands

Following the fall of Napoleon Bonaparte and the Congress of Vienna in 1815, Europe was in a state of flux, with borders being redrawn and nations emerging or reemerging from the turmoil of the Napoleonic Era. The Kingdom of the Netherlands, a newly created state, emerged as a significant player in this post-Napoleonic landscape.

The United Kingdom of the Netherlands, established in 1815, was a political entity that brought together the former Dutch Republic and the Southern Netherlands (present-day Belgium) into a single kingdom. The union was intended to create a buffer state in the Low Countries, maintain peace and stability in the region, and counterbalance the influence of France.

The new kingdom was ruled by William I, also known as William of Orange-Nassau, who had been a prince of the House of Orange and a stadtholder of the Dutch Republic during the late 18th century. As King William I, he sought to consolidate his rule and oversee the reintegration of the Southern Netherlands into the Dutch state.

However, the union between the northern and southern provinces proved to be fraught with challenges. The two regions had distinct linguistic, religious, and cultural differences, and tensions simmered beneath the surface. The predominantly Catholic and French-speaking Southern Netherlands had different aspirations and grievances from the predominantly Protestant and Dutch-speaking northern provinces.

One of the major sources of tension was religion. The Southern Netherlands had been under French rule during

84

the Napoleonic Era and had experienced significant religious reforms and secularization. When the Dutch Reformed Church was reestablished in the south, it created friction with the Catholic majority. Additionally, language differences added to the complexities of governance.

Efforts to impose Dutch as the official language and the Dutch Reformed Church as the state religion in the south met with resistance. These tensions eventually culminated in the Belgian Revolution of 1830, triggered by a performance at the Brussels opera house, which escalated into widespread protests and demands for independence.

The Belgian Revolution, which began in August 1830, resulted in the Southern Netherlands breaking away from the United Kingdom of the Netherlands. Belgium declared its independence on October 4, 1830, and the subsequent fighting led to the formal recognition of Belgian independence in 1831. This event marked the end of the United Kingdom of the Netherlands and the emergence of the Kingdom of Belgium as a sovereign nation.

The loss of Belgium was a significant setback for King William I and the Dutch state. The Kingdom of the Netherlands was now reduced to the northern provinces, which became commonly known as the Kingdom of the Netherlands. It continued to exist as a constitutional monarchy under King William I, who abdicated in 1840 in favor of his son, King William II.

The secession of Belgium and the subsequent redrawing of borders left a lasting impact on the political and cultural landscape of both nations. Belgium established its own monarchy, adopted French as its official language, and embraced a distinct national identity. Meanwhile, the Kingdom of the Netherlands, now confined to the northern provinces, continued to evolve as a constitutional monarchy with its own cultural and political identity.

The restoration of Dutch independence in the northern provinces marked the beginning of a period of nation-building and modernization. The Dutch state focused on economic development, industrialization, and colonial expansion, with the Dutch Empire extending its influence to the Dutch East Indies (Indonesia) and other parts of the world.

The Kingdom of the Netherlands continued to evolve throughout the 19th and 20th centuries, adapting to changing political, social, and economic circumstances. It played a significant role in international diplomacy and was a founding member of institutions like the United Nations and the European Union.

Dutch Colonies in the Caribbean

The Dutch Empire, known for its extensive colonial holdings, also had a significant presence in the Caribbean during the Age of Exploration and Colonialism. These Dutch colonies played a pivotal role in the global trade networks of the 17th century and left an indelible mark on the history of the Caribbean islands.

One of the notable Dutch Caribbean colonies was Curaçao, an island located in the southern Caribbean Sea. The Dutch captured Curaçao from the Spanish in 1634 and established a strategic foothold in the region. Curaçao served as a vital trading and logistical hub for the Dutch West India Company (WIC), facilitating commerce and naval operations in the Caribbean.

Curaçao's deep natural harbors, such as Willemstad's St. Anna Bay, made it an ideal location for Dutch naval and commercial activities. The island became a center for the transatlantic slave trade, with enslaved Africans being brought to Curaçao before being transported to other colonies in the Americas.

Another Dutch colony in the Caribbean was Aruba, situated just off the northern coast of Venezuela. Aruba, like Curaçao, had strategic importance due to its location. It served as a trading post and supply depot for Dutch ships traveling between Europe and the Americas.

Bonaire, located east of Curaçao, was another Dutch possession in the Caribbean. The island was used for salt production, which was a valuable commodity in the 17th century. Bonaire's salt pans were operated by enslaved Africans who toiled in harsh conditions to extract and process the salt.

St. Eustatius, often referred to as Statia, was another Dutch Caribbean colony. The island's main town, Oranjestad, was a bustling trading port. St. Eustatius gained fame as the "Golden Rock" due to its role in the American Revolutionary War. It served as a haven for American privateers and provided military supplies to the American colonies fighting for independence from Britain.

Saba, a small volcanic island in the northeastern Caribbean, was also under Dutch control. Despite its limited size and resources, Saba was home to a resilient population that engaged in agriculture and seafaring.

St. Martin, divided between the French and the Dutch, represented the dual colonial influence in the Caribbean. The Dutch part of St. Martin, known as Sint Maarten, had a significant impact on the island's development. Philipsburg, the capital of Sint Maarten, was a bustling port and center for trade.

Dutch colonial activities in the Caribbean were not limited to commerce. Plantations, primarily focused on sugar and tobacco production, were established on several islands. Enslaved Africans provided the labor necessary for these plantations to thrive, leading to the growth of the African diaspora in the region.

The Dutch Caribbean colonies also witnessed a rich cultural exchange. The Dutch, along with the indigenous populations and enslaved Africans, contributed to the multicultural tapestry of the Caribbean. Elements of Dutch culture, architecture, and language left lasting imprints on these islands.

Over time, the Dutch Caribbean colonies went through various changes, including shifts in colonial administration and economic fortunes. Some islands remained under Dutch control, while others changed hands or achieved independence.

Today, the legacy of Dutch colonialism is visible in the Caribbean through architectural remnants, place names, and cultural influences. The complex history of these Dutch colonies in the Caribbean serves as a reminder of the interconnectedness of the global colonial era and its enduring impact on the region.

World War II and the Dutch Resistance

World War II, one of the most devastating conflicts in history, had a profound impact on the Netherlands and the resilience of its people. As the war unfolded, the Dutch found themselves caught in the crossfire of global events, facing occupation, oppression, and the daunting challenge of resistance.

The Netherlands' involvement in World War II began with the German invasion on May 10, 1940. The swift and overwhelming German offensive quickly overran the Dutch defenses, leading to the surrender of the Netherlands just five days later. The Dutch royal family and government fled to London, where they would establish a government-in-exile.

Under German occupation, life in the Netherlands underwent dramatic changes. The Dutch people faced food shortages, rationing, and restrictions on civil liberties. The occupiers enforced strict regulations, and the Dutch population grappled with the daily challenges of surviving in a war-torn nation.

The Dutch economy was heavily exploited by the Nazis. Industries were repurposed to serve German war efforts, and Dutch workers were subjected to forced labor in factories and farms. The Jewish population of the Netherlands faced the horrors of Nazi persecution, with many being deported to concentration and extermination camps.

Amid these dire circumstances, resistance movements emerged. The Dutch Resistance, or "De Nederlandse Binnenlandse Strijdkrachten," was a network of individuals and groups determined to resist the Nazi occupation. It encompassed a wide spectrum of activities, from distributing illegal newspapers to acts of sabotage and espionage.

The Resistance relied on a vast underground network of couriers, safe houses, and sympathetic citizens. One of the most notable figures in the Dutch Resistance was George Maduro, who would later become the namesake of Madurodam, a miniature city in the Netherlands. Maduro was a law student who joined the resistance and was eventually captured by the Nazis, dying in Dachau concentration camp.

Another significant aspect of the Dutch Resistance was its role in aiding downed Allied pilots. Dutch civilians risked their lives to shelter and guide these pilots to safety, often through a clandestine network known as the "Comet Line." The bravery of these individuals saved many lives and played a vital role in the war effort.

The Dutch Resistance also carried out acts of sabotage. Rail lines were sabotaged, and government buildings were attacked to disrupt German operations. One of the most iconic acts of resistance occurred in February 1945 when a group of Dutch citizens in Amsterdam staged a strike against the German occupiers, leading to violent clashes with German forces.

As the war entered its final stages, the Dutch Resistance played a pivotal role in assisting the Allied forces. They provided valuable intelligence, conducted sabotage missions, and supported the liberation efforts.

The liberation of the Netherlands began in September 1944 when Allied forces, primarily Canadian, launched Operation Market Garden. The liberation of cities like Eindhoven and Nijmegen marked the beginning of the end of German occupation. The iconic Battle of Arnhem, depicted in the movie "A Bridge Too Far," was a significant part of this campaign.

However, it was not until May 5, 1945, that the entire Netherlands was liberated. Canadian troops played a central role in liberating the western part of the country, while other Allied forces, including American and British troops, liberated the south and east. The Dutch people celebrated Liberation Day on May 5, a national holiday that commemorates the end of the Nazi occupation.

World War II had taken a heavy toll on the Netherlands. Thousands of Dutch citizens had lost their lives, and the country faced the daunting task of rebuilding. The Dutch Resistance's role in the war effort was honored, and those who had risked their lives for the cause were celebrated as heroes.

In the post-war period, the Netherlands played a vital role in the reconstruction of Europe and the establishment of international organizations like the United Nations. The memory of World War II and the Dutch Resistance continues to shape the nation's identity and its commitment to the principles of peace, freedom, and human rights.

Post-War Reconstruction and Economic Miracle

The aftermath of World War II left Europe in ruins, and the Netherlands was no exception. However, in the face of devastation, the Dutch people displayed remarkable resilience and determination as they embarked on a journey of post-war reconstruction that would ultimately lead to an economic miracle.

The end of World War II in 1945 marked a turning point for the Netherlands. The country had suffered immense damage, both in terms of infrastructure and human loss. Cities had been bombed, and the Dutch economy was in shambles. But from the ashes of destruction, a collective spirit of rebuilding emerged.

One of the immediate challenges was addressing the widespread housing shortage. Many Dutch cities had suffered significant damage during the war, and thousands were left homeless. The Dutch government initiated large-scale housing projects to provide shelter for those in need. The concept of "wederopbouw," or post-war reconstruction, became a guiding principle.

The Marshall Plan, a U.S. initiative aimed at aiding the recovery of Western Europe, provided vital financial support to the Netherlands and other European nations. The funds were used to kickstart the Dutch economy and rebuild essential infrastructure, including roads, bridges, and ports. The Marshall Plan played a crucial role in jumpstarting the Dutch post-war recovery.

Another pivotal factor in the Dutch economic revival was the establishment of the European Coal and Steel Community (ECSC) in 1951, which laid the groundwork for what would become the European Union. The ECSC promoted economic cooperation and integration, allowing the Netherlands to benefit from increased trade with its European neighbors.

Dutch agriculture also underwent significant changes during the post-war years. The mechanization of farming practices and the introduction of modern agricultural techniques increased productivity. The Netherlands became known for its innovative approaches to agriculture, including the development of high-yield crops and efficient farming methods.

The Port of Rotterdam, one of the largest and busiest ports in the world, played a pivotal role in the Dutch economic recovery. Its strategic location and state-of-the-art facilities made it a hub for international trade. The expansion and modernization of the port further boosted the Dutch economy.

The Netherlands also benefited from the discovery of natural gas reserves in the province of Groningen in 1959. The exploitation of these reserves led to a significant increase in energy production and revenue, contributing to the nation's economic growth.

One of the most remarkable aspects of the Dutch post-war reconstruction was the development of a social welfare system that prioritized healthcare, education, and social security. The Dutch government introduced policies that aimed to provide a safety net for its citizens, ensuring that even during times of economic hardship, basic needs were met.

Education played a vital role in the Netherlands' post-war recovery. The Dutch government invested heavily in education, ensuring that the workforce was well-trained and skilled. The emphasis on education contributed to the country's ability to adapt to new technologies and industries.

The Dutch economic miracle, often referred to as the "Wirtschaftswunder," led to a period of unprecedented prosperity. By the 1960s, the Netherlands had experienced remarkable economic growth, low unemployment rates, and a high standard of living.

The emergence of major Dutch multinational corporations, such as Royal Dutch Shell and Philips, played a significant role in the country's economic success. These companies expanded their operations globally, contributing to the Dutch economy and reinforcing the Netherlands' reputation as a trading nation.

The Dutch economic model, characterized by a strong welfare state, a high degree of economic freedom, and a focus on innovation and education, continued to thrive in the decades that followed. The Dutch economy remained resilient, even in the face of global economic challenges.

The Dutch Royal Family: House of Orange-Nassau

The Dutch Royal Family, also known as the House of Orange-Nassau, holds a prominent place in the history and identity of the Netherlands. With a lineage that dates back centuries, the House of Orange-Nassau has played a significant role in shaping the nation and maintaining its royal traditions.

The House of Orange-Nassau originated in the 16th century, and its name is derived from the ancestral principality of Orange, located in what is now southern France. The house's founding member, William I of Orange (Willem van Oranje), known as William the Silent, emerged as a key figure in the Dutch Revolt against Spanish Habsburg rule in the late 16th century.

William the Silent's leadership and determination to secure the Dutch provinces' independence from Spain made him a national hero. He is often referred to as the "Father of the Fatherland" and is remembered for his pivotal role in establishing the Dutch Republic.

The House of Orange-Nassau's association with the Dutch struggle for independence led to the adoption of the color orange as a symbol of Dutch nationalism. The Dutch national flag, which consists of red, white, and blue horizontal stripes, is known as the "Prinsenvlag" (Prince's Flag) and features orange at the top, representing the House of Orange.

After William the Silent's assassination in 1584, his son, Maurice of Nassau (Maurits van Oranje), succeeded him as Stadtholder of the Dutch Republic. Maurice continued his father's efforts to secure Dutch independence and establish the republic as a formidable European power.

The House of Orange-Nassau's influence extended beyond the borders of the Dutch Republic. In 1689, William III of Orange, also known as William of Orange, became King of England, Scotland, and Ireland as part of the Glorious Revolution. His reign had a profound impact on British constitutional history.

In the 19th century, the House of Orange-Nassau faced significant political changes in the Netherlands. The Dutch monarchy was established in 1815 with the Congress of Vienna, and William I of the House of Orange-Nassau became the first King of the Netherlands. This marked the House of Orange-Nassau's transition from stadtholdership to monarchy.

However, the 19th and early 20th centuries were marked by political turmoil and changes in the Dutch monarchy. The House of Orange-Nassau faced moments of crisis, abdications, and shifts in the monarchy's role within the Dutch constitutional system.

One of the most iconic figures in the House of Orange-Nassau's modern history is Queen Wilhelmina (1890-1948). She ascended to the throne as a young queen in 1890 and played a crucial role during World War II. Her broadcasts to the Dutch people from London during the Nazi occupation earned her the nickname "Radio Oranje."

After World War II, Queen Wilhelmina abdicated in favor of her daughter, Queen Juliana. The Dutch royal family continued to evolve, adapting to the changing role of the monarchy in Dutch society. Queen Juliana and her husband, Prince Bernhard, were widely respected during their reign.

In 1980, Queen Juliana abdicated in favor of her daughter, Queen Beatrix, marking the first time in Dutch history that three consecutive queens had ruled. Queen Beatrix's reign witnessed significant social and political changes in the Netherlands, including the legalization of same-sex marriage.

In 2013, Queen Beatrix abdicated in favor of her eldest son, King Willem-Alexander. King Willem-Alexander and Queen Máxima have been instrumental in representing the Netherlands on the international stage and maintaining the Dutch monarchy's relevance in the 21st century.

The Dutch Royal Family, the House of Orange-Nassau, remains an integral part of Dutch identity and tradition. Their role is largely ceremonial and symbolic, representing continuity and unity in the Netherlands. The royal family's public engagements, official duties, and charitable work continue to be of great importance to the Dutch people.

Modern Dutch Politics and Welfare State

Modern Dutch politics and the development of the welfare state have been characterized by a commitment to social welfare, political pragmatism, and a robust parliamentary democracy. The Netherlands, often seen as a model of progressive and inclusive governance, has evolved over the years to become a nation known for its social policies, economic stability, and commitment to individual rights.

The post-World War II era in the Netherlands was marked by significant political changes. The devastation of the war had left the Dutch people with a strong desire for social and economic stability. This period saw the emergence of the Dutch welfare state, a comprehensive system aimed at providing citizens with healthcare, education, and social security.

The welfare state in the Netherlands is often referred to as the "Polder Model," a term that reflects the nation's tradition of consensus-based policymaking. The Polder Model involves negotiations and cooperation among government, employers, and labor unions to ensure that social and economic policies are fair and balanced.

One of the key architects of the Dutch welfare state was Willem Drees, who served as Prime Minister from 1948 to 1958. Drees implemented social reforms that laid the foundation for the modern Dutch welfare system. His government introduced measures such as universal healthcare and the AOW (Algemene Ouderdomswet), a state pension system for the elderly.

The Dutch healthcare system is known for its accessibility and high quality. It is based on a system of mandatory health insurance, with both public and private insurers.

Citizens are required to have health insurance, and the government provides subsidies to ensure that healthcare remains affordable for all. This approach has resulted in excellent healthcare outcomes and low levels of medical debt.

Education in the Netherlands is also a fundamental aspect of the welfare state. The Dutch education system is characterized by a commitment to equality and accessibility. Education is compulsory until the age of 18, and the government heavily subsidizes both public and private schools. This ensures that children receive quality education regardless of their socio-economic background.

The Dutch political landscape is characterized by a multi-party system. Unlike many countries with two dominant parties, the Netherlands has a plethora of political parties that compete for seats in the Tweede Kamer (House of Representatives). Proportional representation ensures that parties with diverse ideologies have a voice in the political process.

The most well-known Dutch political party is the People's Party for Freedom and Democracy (Volkspartij voor Vrijheid en Democratie, VVD), a center-right party that has been a dominant force in Dutch politics. The Christian Democratic Appeal (Christen-Democratisch Appèl, CDA) and the social-democratic Labour Party (Partij van de Arbeid, PvdA) have also played significant roles in Dutch governance.

Coalition governments are the norm in the Netherlands due to the multi-party system. Forming a coalition requires negotiation and compromise among several parties, resulting in a consensus-based approach to policymaking. This approach, while sometimes seen as slow, contributes to political stability and inclusivity.

The Dutch commitment to individual rights and social inclusivity is evident in its progressive policies. The Netherlands was one of the first countries to legalize same-sex marriage in 2001, and it has consistently ranked high in international indexes of LGBTQ+ rights and gender equality.

Economic stability is another hallmark of modern Dutch politics. The country has a strong, export-oriented economy with a focus on trade, technology, and innovation. The Netherlands is known for its open economy and is home to numerous multinational corporations.

In recent years, climate change and sustainability have become significant political issues in the Netherlands. The Dutch government has implemented policies to address climate change, including ambitious targets for reducing greenhouse gas emissions and transitioning to renewable energy sources.

Modern Dutch politics continue to evolve, reflecting the changing needs and values of Dutch society. The Netherlands remains committed to the principles of social welfare, inclusivity, and individual rights, making it a unique and progressive nation in the global political landscape.

Windmills, Wooden Shoes, and Dutch Traditions

When one thinks of the Netherlands, a vivid image often comes to mind – that of iconic windmills gracefully turning their colossal blades against a backdrop of serene Dutch landscapes. Windmills are not just picturesque symbols; they are an integral part of Dutch heritage, showcasing the Dutch people's ingenuity in harnessing the power of the wind.

Historically, windmills served a multitude of functions. From grinding grain to pumping water, windmills were the workhorses of Dutch agriculture and industry. They played a crucial role in reclaiming land from the sea, allowing the Dutch to expand and protect their low-lying territories.

The Netherlands boasts an impressive array of windmills, and some of the most famous can be found in Kinderdijk. Here, a UNESCO World Heritage Site, 19 windmills stand as a testament to the Dutch mastery of hydraulic engineering. These windmills were used to drain excess water from the polders, creating fertile land for farming.

Another iconic Dutch symbol is the humble wooden shoe, or "klomp" in Dutch. Wooden shoes have a long history in the Netherlands, dating back centuries. These sturdy clogs were originally crafted for practical purposes, providing protection and comfort to Dutch farmers and laborers. Today, they are often seen as a cultural emblem, and some artisans continue to make them by hand.

The Dutch have a rich tradition of craftsmanship, and this extends to the creation of Delftware, a type of blue and white pottery that originated in the city of Delft. Delftware is known for its intricate designs, often featuring scenes of

Dutch life and landscapes. Collectors and enthusiasts treasure these beautiful pieces of ceramic art.

One of the most beloved Dutch traditions is that of Sinterklaas, the Dutch equivalent of Santa Claus. Sinterklaas arrives in the Netherlands in mid-November, accompanied by his helpers known as "Zwarte Pieten" (Black Petes). The celebration of Sinterklaas on December 5th is a cherished holiday for Dutch children, who eagerly await gifts and sweets left by Sinterklaas and his helpers.

The Dutch also have a deep connection to cycling. Bicycles are a common mode of transportation, and the Netherlands boasts an extensive network of bike paths. Dutch cities are designed with cyclists in mind, making it a bike-friendly nation. The love for cycling culminates in annual events like the Tour de France's Grand Depart, which has started in Dutch cities on several occasions.

Cheese is another integral part of Dutch culture, with the Netherlands being famous for its cheese production. Dutch cheeses like Gouda and Edam are renowned worldwide for their quality and taste. Cheese markets, such as the one in Alkmaar, provide a glimpse into the Dutch cheese-making tradition and offer visitors the chance to sample and purchase a variety of cheeses.

Traditional Dutch clothing, although not commonly worn in everyday life, remains a symbol of cultural identity. The most recognizable item is the Dutch cap or bonnet, often seen on women in traditional attire. Regional variations in clothing and headwear reflect the diversity of Dutch culture.

Dutch folk music, known as "Nederlandse Volksmuziek," is deeply rooted in Dutch heritage. Instruments like the accordion and the fiddle are commonly used in traditional

Dutch music. Folk songs often revolve around themes of love, nature, and daily life in the Netherlands.

Dutch festivals and celebrations are a vibrant reflection of Dutch traditions. King's Day (Koningsdag) on April 27th is a nationwide celebration of the Dutch monarch's birthday. On this day, the country turns orange as people participate in various festivities, including flea markets, parades, and outdoor concerts.

In conclusion, windmills, wooden shoes, and Dutch traditions are not just nostalgic symbols but living facets of Dutch culture. They embody the Dutch people's deep connection to their history, their commitment to preserving their heritage, and their ability to blend tradition with modernity seamlessly. These cultural elements continue to shape the Netherlands' identity and captivate the world's imagination.

Dutch Wildlife: From Dunes to Wetlands

The Netherlands, with its diverse landscapes, offers a rich tapestry of wildlife that has adapted to the country's unique habitats. From the coastal dunes to the sprawling wetlands, Dutch wildlife showcases the resilience and adaptability of species in the face of changing environments.

Starting along the North Sea coast, the Dutch dunes are home to a variety of plant and animal species. These sand dunes are not only vital for protecting the low-lying hinterlands from the sea but also serve as a haven for wildlife. Plant species like beach grasses and sea buckthorn have adapted to the harsh conditions, stabilizing the dunes and providing habitat for animals.

Birdlife in the dunes is particularly diverse. Seabirds like the common tern and ringed plover nest on sandy beaches, while the European herring gull is a familiar sight along the coast. Inland, the dunes give way to forests and grasslands where species like the European rabbit and red fox thrive.

Moving inland, the Dutch landscape is crisscrossed by rivers, canals, and waterways. These water bodies are home to an array of aquatic life, including fish like pike, perch, and eel. The European otter, once on the brink of extinction in the Netherlands, has made a remarkable comeback thanks to conservation efforts and improved water quality.

Wetlands play a crucial role in Dutch wildlife conservation. The Wadden Sea, a UNESCO World Heritage Site, is a vast intertidal zone that stretches from the Netherlands to Germany and Denmark. It is a haven for migratory birds, providing a critical stopover point along their journeys. Species like the red knot, Eurasian spoonbill, and Brent goose rely on the Wadden Sea's rich mudflats for feeding.

Inland wetlands, such as the Biesbosch National Park, are a sanctuary for waterfowl and marshland birds. The Eurasian bittern, great egret, and bearded reedling find refuge in these reedbeds and wetlands. The Dutch landscape is dotted with lakes and ponds, where amphibians like the European common frog and the European fire-bellied toad thrive.

Forests in the Netherlands are teeming with life, too. The Dutch beech forests are home to an abundance of bird species, including the Eurasian nuthatch and the European crested tit. Mammals like the European badger and European roe deer can be spotted in the wooded areas.

One of the most iconic Dutch animals is the red deer, which finds its habitat in the Hoge Veluwe National Park and other woodland areas. The Hoge Veluwe is also home to a population of wild boar. These majestic creatures are a testament to the success of Dutch conservation efforts.

The Dutch coastline is a prime location for seals, with both common seals and grey seals calling the Wadden Sea and the Delta region home. Seals have become a symbol of successful marine conservation in the Netherlands.

In recent years, Dutch efforts to reintroduce species like the beaver and the white-tailed eagle have been met with success. These reintroductions have enhanced biodiversity and reinvigorated Dutch ecosystems.

Conservation and habitat restoration remain a priority in the Netherlands to protect and preserve its unique wildlife. The Dutch people's appreciation for nature and their commitment to sustainable practices ensure that Dutch wildlife continues to thrive amidst the challenges of the modern world. Dutch wildlife is not only a testament to the country's natural beauty but also a source of pride for its inhabitants, who work tirelessly to safeguard their natural heritage.

Dutch Cuisine: Beyond Cheese and Tulips

Dutch cuisine, often overshadowed by its famous cheese and iconic tulips, is a culinary journey that reflects the nation's rich history, geography, and traditions. Beyond the stereotypes, Dutch food offers a diverse palette of flavors that tell a story of resilience and innovation.

Cheese is undoubtedly one of the cornerstones of Dutch gastronomy. The Netherlands is renowned for its high-quality cheeses, with Gouda and Edam being the most famous varieties. Dutch cheese-making dates back centuries, and the country's dairy farms produce an array of cheese types, from young and mild to aged and pungent.

Accompanying cheese in the hearts of the Dutch are herring and other seafood. Raw herring, often served with onions and pickles, is a traditional Dutch delicacy. The Dutch take great pride in their herring traditions, and the herring season is eagerly awaited each year. Smoked eel is another seafood favorite, enjoyed in various forms, including in sandwiches or as a gourmet dish.

Pancakes, known as "pannenkoeken," are a beloved Dutch comfort food. These thin, large pancakes come in sweet and savory varieties, with toppings ranging from syrup and powdered sugar to bacon and cheese. Poffertjes, small fluffy pancakes served with butter and powdered sugar, are also popular street food.

Dutch bread, particularly whole-grain varieties, is a staple in Dutch households. Dutch people have a preference for hearty, dense bread with seeds and grains, often enjoyed with cheeses, spreads, or cold cuts. Roggebrood, a dense rye bread, is a traditional favorite.

Dutch pastries and sweets add a touch of indulgence to the cuisine. Stroopwafels, thin waffle-like cookies with a caramel-like syrup filling, are a delightful treat. Appeltaart (apple pie) and gevulde koeken (almond-filled cookies) are other sweet indulgences that can be found in Dutch bakeries.

Indonesia's influence on Dutch cuisine is significant due to the colonial history. This fusion has given birth to the Dutch-Indonesian or "Indo" cuisine. Dishes like nasi goreng (fried rice) and satay are Dutch favorites, and the use of spices and herbs adds complexity to many Dutch dishes. The Netherlands is home to a vibrant market culture, with fresh produce, flowers, and food stalls gracing the streets. One of the most famous food markets is the Albert Cuyp Market in Amsterdam, where locals and tourists can explore a diverse range of street foods and fresh ingredients.

Traditional Dutch cuisine also includes hearty meat-based dishes. Stamppot, a dish made from mashed potatoes and vegetables like kale or sauerkraut, is a comfort food enjoyed during the colder months. Hutspot, a similar dish made with carrots and onions, has historical significance in Dutch culture.

Dutch beer, particularly lagers and pilsners, is a favorite beverage. The Netherlands has a thriving beer culture, with breweries crafting a wide range of beer styles. Dutch gin, known as jenever, has a long history and is experiencing a resurgence in popularity. In recent years, Dutch cuisine has seen a resurgence in interest in local and sustainable ingredients. Farm-to-table dining is becoming more prevalent, with restaurants showcasing Dutch-grown produce and artisanal products.

While Dutch cuisine may not be as internationally famous as some of its European counterparts, it is a reflection of the country's history, culture, and adaptability. Dutch chefs and food enthusiasts are continually reimagining traditional dishes, infusing new life into the culinary scene. Dutch cuisine is a delightful journey through flavors that are both comforting and unexpected, making it a worthy exploration for any food lover.

Iconic Dutch Tourist Sights: Windmills, Canals, and Tulip Fields

The Netherlands, with its picturesque landscapes and charming cities, boasts a plethora of iconic tourist sights that have captured the imaginations of travelers for generations. From the gently turning windmills in the countryside to the intricate canal networks of historic cities and the vibrant fields of blooming tulips, these sights are emblematic of the Dutch experience.

Windmills stand as enduring symbols of Dutch engineering prowess and ingenuity. These iconic structures, with their colossal sails turning gracefully in the wind, have become synonymous with the Netherlands. The windmill's history in the Dutch landscape dates back to the 12th century when they were initially developed to pump water out of low-lying polders, helping to reclaim land from the sea and prevent flooding. Today, windmills can be found throughout the country, serving various functions. The windmills of Kinderdijk, a UNESCO World Heritage Site, are among the most famous, showcasing the Dutch mastery of hydraulic engineering. Visitors can explore this enchanting landscape, marveling at the 19 windmills that continue to maintain the delicate balance between land and water.

Amsterdam, the capital city, is renowned for its intricate canal system. The historic center of Amsterdam, a UNESCO World Heritage Site, features a network of canals, bridges, and charming 17th-century houses that create a postcard-perfect setting. Canal cruises are a popular way to explore the city, allowing visitors to glide past iconic landmarks like the Anne Frank House and the Rijksmuseum. The canal belt reflects Amsterdam's Golden

Age, when the city flourished as a center of trade and culture.

Tulip fields in the Netherlands are a kaleidoscope of colors that burst into life during the spring season. The Dutch have a deep affinity for tulips, which were originally introduced to the country in the 16th century. Keukenhof Gardens, often referred to as the "Garden of Europe," is one of the world's largest flower gardens and a showcase for Dutch horticultural expertise. Here, millions of tulips, along with other spring blooms, create a breathtaking spectacle. The annual Keukenhof Tulip Festival attracts visitors from around the globe, who come to witness the vibrant fields in full bloom.

The historic city of Delft, known for its blue and white pottery, is another must-visit destination. The charming canalside city is home to the Royal Delft Porcelain Factory, where visitors can learn about the craft of Delftware production and explore the museum's collection of exquisite ceramics.

Zaanse Schans, located just outside Amsterdam, offers a glimpse into Dutch history and craftsmanship. This open-air museum showcases well-preserved historic windmills, wooden houses, and artisan workshops. Visitors can witness traditional Dutch crafts in action, from wooden clog making to cheese production.

The medieval city of Utrecht, with its iconic Dom Tower, is a hidden gem that invites exploration. Climbing the Dom Tower's 465 steps rewards visitors with panoramic views of the city and its charming canals.

Giethoorn, often called the "Venice of the North," is a serene village with no roads, where picturesque canals are the primary means of transportation. Visitors can navigate the waterways by renting a traditional Dutch "whisper boat" or simply enjoy the tranquil atmosphere.

The Van Gogh Museum in Amsterdam and the Kröller-Müller Museum in Hoge Veluwe National Park provide art enthusiasts with the opportunity to immerse themselves in the works of Dutch masters, including Vincent van Gogh.

These iconic Dutch tourist sights, from windmills and canals to tulip fields and historic cities, offer a captivating journey through the Netherlands' rich cultural heritage and natural beauty. They are testaments to the Dutch people's commitment to preserving their traditions and sharing their unique way of life with the world.

Amsterdam: The Venice of the North

Amsterdam, often referred to as the "Venice of the North," is a city of captivating beauty and historical significance. This epithet is not merely a poetic comparison; it speaks to the city's intricate network of canals and waterways, its rich cultural heritage, and its unique place in the world.

The canals of Amsterdam are the lifeblood of the city, weaving through its fabric like veins in a body. They form a complex web that has earned the city its nickname. In fact, the city boasts more than 100 kilometers (60 miles) of canals, over 1,500 bridges, and a harmonious blend of architectural styles that span centuries. These canals are not just scenic waterways; they are the result of meticulous urban planning and hydraulic engineering that date back to the 17th century.

The famous Canal Ring, or Grachtengordel, is a UNESCO World Heritage Site and the heart of Amsterdam's canal system. This semi-circular network consists of three main canals: Herengracht (Gentlemen's Canal), Keizersgracht (Emperor's Canal), and Prinsengracht (Prince's Canal). Along these picturesque waterways, you'll find stunning canal houses adorned with distinctive gables and elegant facades. These houses, many of which were built during the Dutch Golden Age, reflect the city's historical prosperity and its enduring commitment to architectural beauty.

One of the most iconic images of Amsterdam is the houseboats that line its canals. These floating residences, often adorned with colorful flowers and unique personal touches, are a testament to the city's creativity and adaptability. Living on the water is a cherished part of Amsterdam's culture, and houseboat communities are an integral part of the city's social fabric.

The canals serve practical purposes as well. They were originally constructed for transportation and defense, and today they continue to fulfill these roles. Canal cruises are a popular way for visitors to explore Amsterdam, offering a leisurely journey through the city's history and architecture. The canals are also used for water management, helping to regulate water levels and prevent flooding in this low-lying land.

Amsterdam's canal-side neighborhoods are brimming with character. The Jordaan district, once a working-class area, is now a vibrant hub of art galleries, cozy cafes, and boutiques. The Grachtengordel, with its grand houses, is a testament to the opulence of the Dutch Golden Age. The De Pijp neighborhood is a lively district known for its markets, restaurants, and the famous Albert Cuyp Market.

The Anne Frank House, located along the Prinsengracht, is a poignant reminder of the city's wartime history. It is the hiding place where Anne Frank, a Jewish girl, wrote her diary during World War II. The museum preserves this history, allowing visitors to reflect on the resilience of the human spirit even in the darkest of times.

Amsterdam's cultural riches are equally impressive. The Rijksmuseum, Van Gogh Museum, and Stedelijk Museum are renowned institutions that house world-class collections of art and history. Rembrandt's masterpiece, "The Night Watch," finds its home in the Rijksmuseum, while the Van Gogh Museum showcases the works of the iconic Dutch painter.

The city's vibrant nightlife, diverse culinary scene, and welcoming atmosphere make Amsterdam a destination that offers something for every traveler. From the lively streets of the Red Light District to the peaceful Vondelpark, Amsterdam's charm is boundless.

Amsterdam's moniker as the "Venice of the North" is more than just a picturesque comparison; it encapsulates the essence of a city that has mastered the art of living with and on the water. Its canals are not just waterways; they are the arteries that pump life into a city that thrives on history, culture, and an unwavering connection to its aquatic roots. Amsterdam is a place where the past and the present gracefully coexist, inviting all who visit to become a part of its unique tapestry.

Utrecht, Rotterdam, and Historic City Centers

Utrecht, Rotterdam, and the historic city centers scattered across the Netherlands offer a captivating glimpse into the country's rich and diverse history. Each of these urban centers tells a unique story, blending the old with the new in a captivating tapestry of architecture, culture, and innovation.

Utrecht, one of the oldest cities in the Netherlands, boasts a historic city center that is both picturesque and bustling with life. The city is often referred to as "Domstad" due to the iconic Dom Tower, which dominates the skyline. Standing at 112 meters (367 feet), the Dom Tower is the tallest church tower in the Netherlands and serves as a symbol of Utrecht. Visitors can climb its 465 steps for panoramic views of the city and the surrounding region.

The heart of Utrecht is characterized by charming canals lined with cafés, restaurants, and shops. The Oudegracht, or Old Canal, is particularly enchanting, featuring unique wharf cellars that have been transformed into vibrant businesses. Strolling along the canals and crossing the many bridges that crisscross the waterways offers a glimpse into the city's medieval past.

Rotterdam, on the other hand, is a testament to resilience and innovation. Once heavily bombed during World War II, Rotterdam rose from the ashes to become a modern architectural marvel. The city's skyline is a testament to its forward-thinking spirit, with iconic structures like the Cube Houses and the Erasmus Bridge capturing the imagination of visitors.

The historic city center of Rotterdam, known as "Delfshaven," is a charming enclave that escaped the destruction of the war. Its picturesque canals, cobbled streets, and historic houses provide a glimpse into the city's past. The Pilgrim Fathers, who later sailed to America on the Mayflower, departed from Delfshaven, adding to its historical significance.

Amsterdam's historic city center, often referred to as the "Old Center" or "Centrum," is an enchanting maze of narrow streets, canals, and historic buildings. The Royal Palace, originally built as the city's Town Hall during the Dutch Golden Age, stands as a grand architectural masterpiece on Dam Square. The Anne Frank House, with its poignant history, is another prominent attraction in the heart of the city.

Leiden, known as the "City of Discoveries," is renowned for its historic center and its role in the scientific advancements of the Dutch Golden Age. Leiden University, one of the oldest in the country, was attended by luminaries such as Rembrandt and Descartes. The city's canals and historic buildings contribute to its timeless charm.

Delft, famous for its blue and white pottery, boasts a well-preserved historic center that invites exploration. The Nieuwe Kerk, or New Church, is a prominent feature on the city's skyline, and the Vermeer Center pays homage to the renowned painter Johannes Vermeer.

The Hague, the political capital of the Netherlands, is home to a historic city center with an array of historic buildings, including the Binnenhof, where the Dutch government meets. The city's international character is reflected in its diverse neighborhoods and cultural attractions.

Maastricht, nestled in the southern part of the Netherlands, features a historic city center with a distinctly European ambiance. The city's Roman origins are evident in the architecture, and the Vrijthof Square is a lively hub of cultural events.

These cities and their historic centers are not frozen in time; they are vibrant hubs where the past and present coexist harmoniously. Whether exploring the medieval canals of Utrecht, admiring the modern skyline of Rotterdam, or wandering through the charming streets of Amsterdam, visitors to the Netherlands are treated to a rich tapestry of history and culture that continues to evolve and inspire.

Conclusion

The history of the Netherlands is a story of resilience, innovation, and cultural richness that has left an indelible mark on the world stage. From its ancient roots as a land of marshes and rivers to its rise as a global trading power during the Dutch Golden Age, the Netherlands has continually evolved, adapting to the challenges of nature and history.

The early inhabitants, from hunter-gatherers to settlers, laid the foundation for the Dutch identity. The rise of ancient Dutch tribes like the Batavi and the influence of Roman rule left lasting imprints on the land and its people. The Viking invasions and the connection to Charlemagne's Carolingian Empire shaped the course of Dutch history.

In the medieval era, Dutch society was characterized by feudal lords, medieval estates, and the emergence of trade routes through the Hanseatic League. The Golden Age of Dutch cities, with their remarkable prosperity and artistic achievements, showcased the nation's prominence on the world stage.

The Dutch mastered the art of managing water and land, becoming expert dike builders and reclaiming land from the sea. Flanders and the Dutch Renaissance added cultural depth to the Dutch experience, while the Protestant Reformation and the Eighty Years' War led to the birth of Dutch independence.

The Dutch East India Company (VOC) wielded significant global influence, establishing Dutch colonies and trade networks across the world. Dutch exploration and colonization expanded the nation's reach and solidified its position as a maritime power.

Tulip Mania, though a brief and peculiar obsession, is emblematic of the Dutch passion for horticulture and commerce. The Dutch Republic served as a model of republicanism, embracing tolerance and freedom of thought.

The Anglo-Dutch Wars and the Glorious Revolution underscored the Dutch maritime supremacy and the role of William of Orange in English history. The Dutch Empire continued to expand globally, leaving a lasting legacy in places like Indonesia and beyond.

Dutch art, science, and commerce flourished during the Dutch Golden Age, producing renowned figures like Rembrandt. The Scientific Revolution and the contributions of Dutch scholars added to the nation's intellectual prestige.

Dutch literature and philosophy have also played a significant role in shaping the cultural landscape. The Dutch colonial legacy, including its involvement in the Atlantic slave trade, leaves a complex historical legacy to grapple with.

The Napoleonic Era marked a shift from the Dutch Republic to a kingdom under French influence. Independence was later restored with the creation of the Kingdom of the Netherlands.

The Dutch colonies in the Caribbean, with their rich histories and diverse cultures, reflect the nation's global reach. World War II and the Dutch Resistance are part of the nation's wartime narrative.

Post-war reconstruction and the economic miracle catapulted the Netherlands into a modern era of prosperity. The Dutch Royal Family, the House of Orange-Nassau, continues to play a symbolic role in the nation's identity.

Modern Dutch politics and the development of the welfare state reflect the nation's commitment to social progress. Dutch traditions, from windmills and wooden shoes to wildlife and cuisine, embody the essence of Dutch culture.

Iconic tourist sights, such as windmills, canals, and tulip fields, showcase the Netherlands' natural beauty and heritage.

In conclusion, the Netherlands' history is a tapestry woven from the threads of time, reflecting the resilience and innovation of its people. From its ancient roots to its modern achievements, the Netherlands stands as a testament to the enduring spirit of a nation that has left an indelible mark on the world.

Thank you for taking the time to read this book on the history of the Netherlands. We hope you found it informative, engaging, and insightful, as it was our goal to provide you with a comprehensive journey through the rich tapestry of Dutch history.

If you enjoyed reading this book and found it valuable, we kindly ask for your support by leaving a positive review. Your feedback and review will not only be greatly appreciated but will also help others discover and benefit from the content within these pages.

Your support means the world to us, and we look forward to hearing your thoughts and impressions. Thank you once again for choosing to explore the history of the Netherlands with us, and we hope you continue to find inspiration in the fascinating stories of the past.

Printed in Great Britain
by Amazon

42146335R00069